Science and Religion

Science and Religion

A Contemporary Perspective

JOHN M. DUFFEY

RESOURCE *Publications* · Eugene, Oregon

SCIENCE AND RELIGION
A Contemporary Perspective

Copyright © 2013 John M. Duffey. All rights reserved. Except for brief quotations in critical publications or reviews, no part of this book may be reproduced in any manner without prior written permission from the publisher. Write: Permissions, Wipf and Stock Publishers, 199 W. 8th Ave., Suite 3, Eugene, OR 97401.

Resource Publications
An Imprint of Wipf and Stock Publishers
199 W. 8th Ave., Suite 3
Eugene, OR 97401

www.wipfandstock.com

ISBN 13: 978-1-61097-728-9

Produced in the United States of America

This literary work is endorsed by
the Reformist Catholic Church of North America
2012

Approved by the Council of Bishops
Reformist Catholic Church of North America
2012

To all those seeking enlightenment of the divine and His nature . . .

Basic scientific research, as well as applied research, is a significant expression of man's dominion over creation. Science and technology are precious resources when placed at the service of man and promote his integral development for the benefit of all. By themselves however they cannot disclose the meaning of existence and of human progress. Science and technology are ordered to man, from whom they take their origin and development; hence they find in the person and in his moral values both evidence of their purpose and awareness of their limits.

—Catechism of the Catholic Church §2293

Contents

Acknowledgments • *ix*
Introduction • *xi*

PART ONE: DEFINING SCIENCE AND RELIGION
    1 What is Religion? • 3
    2 What is Science? • 69

PART TWO: A ROCKY RELATIONSHIP
    3 Contemporary Perspectives of Relational Science and Religion • 87
    4 Atrocities of Both Science and Religion • 94

PART THREE: A TRULY PERFECT UNION
    5 Religion: Venerator and Giver of Hope • 113
    6 Science: Discoverer and Giver of Comfort • 118

    Conclusion • *122*

Acknowledgments

I would like to give special thanks to the following: first, the Father, the Son, and the Holy Spirit; the holy Trinity in its individual and combined elements has filled me with great insight and enlightenment to observe and report the duality of good and evil in humankind and the complimentary nature of science and spiritual faith. Second, my two lovely children, Heather and John II, who have rendered unconditional love, admiration, and support without which I would surely die. I love them both dearly and thank God for these most precious gifts. Finally, my mother, Nana Duffey, whose support has lifted me in the dreariest of circumstances and carried me through when determination and confidence left me abandoned. She is my hero.

Introduction

FOR AS LONG AS the official process of scientific discovery has been in existence there has been friction between what is discovered by it, the discoverers, and those who have faith in the spiritual world and its traditions. The conflict hasn't remedied itself, either. In fact, the schism and resentment seem to have grown and continue to grow exponentially. Some have even stated that the attempt to unify the two perspectives of understanding regarding the natural and spiritual worlds is, at this point, futile.

Other observers of the adversarial relationship between science and faith believe things are not beyond repair. These individuals believe science is being viewed erroneously as a competitor or replacement to religion when, in fact, it is far from it. Science is a tool. It is a standardized and universal process of thought and discovery that serves to facilitate the achievement of human enlightenment on issues concerning the natural world.

For the scientifically oriented, religion (especially Christianity) is the root of all of humankind's atrocities to itself and the earth. To the spiritually inclined people, science has been the tool and exponential facilitator of man's evil doings to other men and the earth. The truth, however, is most likely in the middle. One must always remember that there is his side, her side, and reality regarding perspectives and situational/conditional accuracy. How can both be in a dance of duality, of good and bad?

The answer to such a question lies in the common denominator for the two fields of belief and enlightenment. Both science and religion are tools and mechanisms used by man to achieve a complete understanding of his origins, present, future, and purpose. Religion, science, and philosophy have been and continue to be the mechanisms by which these four ponderances are addressed. So, where is the problem?

Humanity is what is really at fault for the bad and credit for the good. Humans, all of us, do not like to admit wrongdoing or take personal responsibility for the consequences of wrongdoing. We certainly would not need

Introduction

attorneys if the case was otherwise for us. When people win a race, achieve a great academic goal, bring peace to a region of the world, or invent some medical marvel that lengthens the human lifespan, they are quick to take credit for it and to even jealously guard that credit. But, when people kill, persecute, harass, ostracize, discriminate, withhold charity, or wage brutal war they are quick to justify their actions and lay blame on others. The bottom line is we do not like to take responsibility for our ill doings and will go to great lengths to avoid responsibility.

What do we hear from our brothers and sisters when there is good? We hear, "I won the race," "I achieved this goal," and "I brought peace." What do we never hear them say? We never hear them say: "Thank God for giving me the strength to win this race." "Thanks to my scientific knowledge of human anatomy and biochemistry, I have won this race." "Thank you, Lord, for bringing this success to me." "I am thankful for the scientific method that allowed me to make this discovery." We never give credit to God or science when things are good for us and we have done well. We always take full credit for it while casting both science and religion aside.

What is heard when one kills another, steals from another, wages war and murder against others, or withholds much-needed charity from others? "I killed him because he offended Islam!" "We waged war to free the Holy City from the Muslim infidels!" "I took their things because they are an inferior race and science supports this." "We took their land and trinkets because they were ignorant and weak in trusting us and we wanted their things." "We waged war against the Jews because they are liars and snakes and offend God." "Scientific data proves Iraq is producing and hording weapons of mass destruction." Can you see how both science and religion are being used to justify the evil side of humanity?

What does all this mean? What conclusions should be drawn from these observations—these realizations regarding human nature, character, and the universe it lives in? The examples listed here are not alone, either. There are not thousands but millions of examples throughout the history of mankind where atrocities and ill doings have been done under the false justification of religion, science, or both. Science and religion do not kill people; people kill people.

Like a coin, humans have two sides. We are designed with a duality of good and evil. Not one of us is spared this duality, though one has been born absent of evil (Jesus Christ) and others have been able to meditate away their darker side (such as Buddhists and Hindus). We are proud of the lighter side and ashamed of the darker side. Thus, we all seek to be praised for being good and receive gratification through doing good while we seek to shed responsibility for our evil side and feel ashamed for our darker deeds. In order to evade personal responsibility for our sinful, unethical, and immoral ways, we use religion and science to rationalize and justify them.

Therefore, it is humanity that is responsible for humanity's suffering and not its religion or methodology for discovering the laws of nature. It is our greed, covetousness, lust, desire for power, political ambitions, and intolerance that has led to the atrocities recorded throughout history. Science and religion have been nothing more than tools for the justification of these immoral and wicked doings. The cause, all along, has been human beings and their uncontrolled darker side combined with their rejection of personal responsibility for wrongful ways. Our constructs and conceptualizations are not responsible—we are.

PART ONE

Defining Science and Religion

1

What is Religion?

OVER THE DECADES PEOPLE have often been confused as to what the word, "religion," means. For some, a religious person is a person who believes strongly, not moderately or slightly, in Christ and the Christian doctrine. For others, religion has a broader and more inclusive definition. For these people, religion encompasses all belief systems where there is a consideration of a divine being. Then, there are those in the middle and those who take on strict, but opposite, definitive views. The result has been a complete misunderstanding of what religion is and what being religious means.

RELIGION DEFINED AND DISSECTED

In order to understand religion and its role in humanity's achievements, failures, and suffering one must know the exact definition of the term. Without this complete and solid understanding, a person is lost in the definitive chaos of the world's ignorance. Unfortunately, the ranks of the ignorant among humanity, at all social and economic levels, has grown significantly from generation to generation, allowing for hatred to stew in a pot of uninformed assumptions and ignorant rigidity.

Defining Religion

So, what is religion? How do we discern the correct definition from all the incorrect ones out there? Is it possible to erase or halt hundreds of years of misdefinition, ever-solidifying bias, and social rigidity? Thankfully, to our Lord and Savior Jesus Christ and the Holy Father, it is not too late to stop and repair the damage done by ignorance, social rebellion, and traditional rigidity. We start by identifying the true and most basic definition of religion.

Religion, is generally defined as having three perspective elements. These are cultural belief, social system, and personal belief. For most people, religion is viewed in a very narrow manner through only one of the three perspectives. But, religion is all three and very broad. It is a sort of "trinity." Religion is applicable and related at all three corners of the triangle.

The cultural belief perspective sees religion as a centralized, or common, set of beliefs and traditions related to a particular deity or group of deities. A Central Cultural Identity (CCI) is the cement that holds a society together. Common spiritual beliefs are one of several elements related to a society's central identification. In some parts of the world, neighboring social groups have directly opposing religions in order to enforce their independence and competitiveness with one another.

From this perspective we can see how religion reinforces inter-societal norms and order. It becomes the supreme justification for the culture's laws and ways of interacting with other cultures. In other words, religion is a healthy part of any culture or society when relations by and between various cultures are considered. It is what distinguishes them from all other cultures. Not one cultural group can be seen, in all of recorded history, that is absent of a central or core belief system that is held and supported by the majority membership.

> "Let us trust God, and our better judgment to set us right hereafter. United we stand, divided we fall. Let us not split into factions which must destroy that union upon which our existence hangs."
> —Patrick Henry, 1799

So, is the Central Cultural Identity (CCI) element of Religion bad? It is hardly arguable that there is good in providing a single unifying element that pulls people together. It allows for those of a particular society to unite against foes, struggle together for survival, rescue each other from great danger, and to act in other ways that are collectively beneficial. Is this bad?

This element of religion, the first of three elemental pillars, is what is often misrepresented by the naysayers. These opponents to religion and the religious will often say religion is a mechanism of inter-societal conflict. There is no doubting that many wars have been fought in the name of one religion or another. But, they have been equally fought for one political

What is Religion?

reason or another, too. Behind every religious justification for war has been a political agenda.

However, it is important that one examine the true root for the good and bad done under the auspices of religion. Is religion the root of humankind's compassion and kindness to one another? Is it the root of all the evils humanity has wrought upon itself? Or, is religion, like science and scissors, a mere tool used by humanity to justify their own good and ill will? The root of humankind's woes and worries is humankind, not its religiousness.

Religion rests upon three pillars. The second of these is Social Belief (SB). In this regard, religion becomes the central belief mechanism for a societal construct. It is the common spiritual denominator for a culture and its various subcultures. It is the collective spiritual ideology that binds one to another and advances internal progress and peace. Unlike CCI, the SB perspective illustrates and establishes rules for internal social behavior.

Family values, concepts of justice, marriage, worldviews, mechanisms of governance, and rules of business are all influenced by common religious social beliefs. This, then, becomes the internal glue that prevents factioning and chaos. It is the foundation upon which stability and peaceful resolution within a cultural body are built.

The third element of religion is the Personal Belief System (PBS). Each individual, regardless of their societal or cultural affiliation, develop their own interpretations of the spirit and the spiritual world. It is often influenced by and compatible with the broader SB system, but it includes interpretive elements based on personal, spiritual experience that is not adequately addressed by the broader social definitive element.

An example of this can be seen in the various individual perspectives within the Christian community regarding the returning spirits of those who have died. These spirits are often referred to as ghosts. Their existence and origin are believed or perceived in different ways within the Christian community alone. Some believe that when the body dies the soul is free to wander at will. Others believe the souls rest until called by Jesus Christ during the end times. Although these people adhere to the same general, or social, religious belief system they each hold individual beliefs within the broader system.

Another example of individual belief perspective within the broader social belief system is when individuals spiritually interpret disaster or bad times. One may see it as a challenge to faith; another may believe it is the doing of the devil. A third person may see travesty as divine punishment for living in an offensive or sinful manner. All three of these individual beliefs are constructed within a common social belief system: Christianity.

Religious Categories

The emergence of comparative religion allowed for the philosophical, developmental, historical, and practical elements of human belief to be divided into categories. Comparative religion is the study of human beliefs by time and location. The various religions of the world and its history relate on some points and completely conflict over others. Through comparative study, humanity becomes aware of how contemporary religious thoughts and practices came to be and why there are differences in divine conceptualization, identity, and reverence from one social group to another.

Religion has been divided into categories related to history, geography, size, and techno-cultural advancement. This has been quite useful in understanding both the divine and humankind itself. Religious beliefs and practices tend to correlate to a given peoples' current technological, cultural, and academic levels. While religion is a mere spiritual guideline and/or philosophy in more advanced cultures, it holds a far more concrete and governing presence in the lesser developed cultures of today and yesterday. Its role in a particular culture is determined by that culture's level of technological, physical, and philosophical understanding.

World Religions

Each religion, now and in the past, can be categorized by its size and spread across the globe. World religions—also known as international religions—cross political and cultural boundaries and can be seen in several or even all parts of the world. This further breaks down into global and regional faiths.

Regional religions are international and/or cross-cultural faiths practiced in more than one country but remain generally together on one continent, or sparsely together on a neighboring continent. These are known as regional religions because, when plotted on a map, the religious movement tends to stay collected in a specific geographical area that normally does not exist sporadically around the earth.

Global religions are those that have grown in size and spread to include two or more continents around the earth. These religions have managed to concrete themselves in the area of their origin and have then spread

What is Religion?

over time onto different continents, countries, and even various differing cultural groups around the planet sporadically. As new spiritual and philosophical ideologies permeate, political and social changes are created in the affected societies as old beliefs and norms are replaced with new ones relative to the new faith.

An example of what is global and what is regional can be seen by examining Islam. This Abrahamic faith is, beyond a doubt, global. It can be encountered in all parts of the globe. But, there are numerous sub-faiths or denominations of Islam that are quite regional. For instance, Shia Islam is seen primarily in Iran, Iraq, Afghanistan, and Pakistan while Sunni Islam is seen in Saudi Arabia and other Middle Eastern countries. Another form of Islam is seen solely in Yemen while another is isolated in Pakistan. The Nation of Islam is a hybrid form of Islam found primarily in the United States. Together, they make up the global religion of Islam, but the sub-groups are primarily regional with some exceptions having developed in Sunni and Shia Islamic sects.

Indigenous Religions

Indigenous religions are those belief systems specific to a particular culture and sub-regional area. From the global perspective these religions are seedlings with potential to grow into more globally practiced traditions. But, at present they are quite small and restricted to a particular society.

Some such faiths never manage to go beyond their originating cultures. Many cease to exist when the culture that sustained them dissolves or is overtaken by another culture with conflicting beliefs. In the Americas this can be seen in the rise and fall of the Anasazi, Mayan, and Aztec cultures and religions.

Examples of contemporary indigenous religion can be seen in the spiritual practices of the various Native American peoples in the United States and Canada. These systems are restricted to a particular group of people in a specific area of the region. Its size is restricted to the numerical volume of the supporting culture's population. The religion itself focuses solely on those people and reinforces their social norms and worldview.

Through an examination of cultural history one discovers that the expansion of indigenous, tribal, and restricted religions occurs primarily through conflict and conquest. This is also the primary reason for the coming and going of small societies and their associated belief mechanisms.

Science and Religion

Traditional versus New Religious Movements

At the most basic level, religion is broken down and categorized according to concepts/beliefs, location, timeline position, cultural make-up, and size. In the timeline area we examine a movement's place and span in history while the age area examines how long it has existed. Categorization allows for better analysis and understanding regarding the many different religions, their foundations, practices, beliefs, and even the evolutionary processes. A unique observation can be made in comparing the newer religions and intra-religious movements with the older and more traditional forms.

Traditional religious movements are defined in two ways. The first is by the amount of time they have existed and the second is their closeness in history to the original belief system. As a religion spans across generations it becomes the traditional faith for a particular culture. It is well known that small changes occur from generation to generation and these changes usually build to become a new, but related, belief system. Traditional faiths are the oldest original systems from which, in the normal evolution of things, new things spring. However, even the new movements become traditional with enough time.

Generally, traditional religions are determined through age. A faith system beyond five hundred years in age and active in contemporary times can be categorized as traditional. Many scholars believe the age amount should be increased to at least one thousand years. That being said, a religious concept/practice can become a well-engrained cultural element in just a few generations (e.g., five hundred years).

When a religion completely sputters out and falls into nothing greater than references in history books we call it an extinct or dead religion. Traditional labeling applies to contemporary faiths with long histories only. Long-lasting belief systems that have died out are dead because they are not practiced by any culture in the present.

Are the dead faiths worth knowing and studying? There is absolutely no doubting every society is deeply affected by its primary religious system. Rulers have decided in accordance with religious custom and beliefs. Often the priests or shamans were referenced to render divine guidance on important issues and in the making of the internal governing laws. Down to the lowest member of a given society there are laws and traditions based on spiritual beliefs and interpretations that both comfort and command. When learning about the current societies of the world we are forced to look at those that came before. We look at the root societies to today's cultural formulations. How did we come to be? Where did we come from? Why do we believe what we believe? These are all questions to which answers are sought through the efforts of cultural anthropology, history, and archaeology. One part of understanding current and ancient societies and their developments is to consider that group's religious practices and beliefs. So, should we know and study the bygone religions of man? We certainly should, as this is the only way we can truly understand how we came to be today.

Some examples of traditional religions are Judaism, Christianity, Islam, Buddhism, and Hinduism. These are all quite aged and well-engrained in multiple contemporary cultures. Remember, a traditional faith is older than five hundred years and is well-engrained in one or more contemporary cultural groups. It may have several denominations of varying ages, but it is related in basic belief and practice.

New religious movements are exactly what the label implies. These are either brand new (foreign to all other religions) or a newer variant of an already existing, usually traditional, religious system. Obviously, they are less than five hundred years in age and may or may not be related to an older root religion. Most new religions are simply the same old thing with some additions or subtractions in beliefs and practices. Doctrinal application is often the reason behind a new faith's emergence.

But, there are others that classify as truly new. These are the religions seemingly born from out of the blue. A religious leader or group of people decides the spiritual world is of a way and means not held by any other faith. In today's world we see a seemingly endless string of these types of belief systems sprouting up all over the planet. Scientology is a prime example of a new faith that has developed and remains independent of the traditional mechanisms of belief.

TYPES OF RELIGION

There are as many religious belief systems around the globe and throughout history as there are cultures and culturally specific philosophies. In fact, they often go hand-in-hand from one society to another. Religion is often formulated and expressed in ways that are reflective of the originating culture's ideology, philosophy, and functionality.

Science and Religion

Remember, religion is a human construct purposed for creating understanding and communion with the spiritual realm and to resolve certain conflicts of logic regarding what is seen with what is unseen. Being human-made should not give reason or support to claim there is no spiritual world or deity. Nor does it lend credence to assertions of religion being false or a mechanism for social control. This is because the religious construct is humankind's attempt to define and revere the divine and the nature of the spiritual realm. It facilitates the understanding and interpretation of spiritual matters (that which is but lies beyond the normal restrictions of nature) and is not a fabrication (that which isn't but is asserted as being).

Generally, religions are categorized, or typed, according to what their core beliefs are and how they evolved from or relate to other current or dead religions. Labeling and comparing allows us to understand how religion came to be, how it relates to other contemporary religions, and where spiritual evolution will most likely take human faith and belief in the future.

An example of the relationship of different religions can be seen in reviewing Christianity, Islam, and Judaism. Though they have distinctly different traditions and beliefs they are all rooted in the same, original Judaic faith. All three are considered Abrahamic faiths because they are all rooted in Abraham—they all claim their beginnings there. The Old Testament texts of Christianity, the Torah of contemporary Judaism, and the Qur'an of Islam all contain the same stories of creation and of Abraham.

Does being of the same religious type automatically mean there is peace and agreement by and between the sub-types? Unfortunately, like with family matters, being related doesn't mean there is peace and harmony present. Countless wars and acts of violence have been inflicted, one against the other, throughout history. In the Abrahamic faiths there have been wars between Christians and Jews, Jews and Christians, Muslims and Christians, and Muslim and Jews. Within Christianity alone there have been bloody fights between Roman Catholic and orthodox Catholic. There were also great persecutions and fights between the Catholics and Protestants.

Being of one religion that is related to another does not bring peace and does not mean there is peace and agreement among the sub-types. In fact, the sub-type faiths are often the product of disagreement from within another belief mechanism that results in a schism, or split, between arguing factions. So, before a person goes off declaring religion to be the source of violence and disagreement he/she should more closely examine the means by which the related but different faiths came to be. The disagreement and

What is Religion?

violent opposition of one to another usually precedes the development of religious and/or doctrinal denominations.

Regardless of whether or not certain religious conceptualizations are adversarial they may still share common developmental/historical roots and doctrinal applications. Many Christians, especially within conservative Christianity, oppose the scientific notion of biological evolution while other Christians embrace it. The rejection/acceptance line is drawn along doctrinal and interpretive expressions within Christendom.

There are Christians who deny evolution in the geological and biological sense while being the products of spiritual, intellectual, and social evolution themselves. It is humorous such a condition is considered while reading the religious arguments and condemnations of our scientific brothers and sisters who assert the theory that we are a product of biological evolution. The church, indeed all human belief, changes when new knowledge is gained, socio-political structures change, environments change, and new interpretations emerge to meet contemporary spiritual challenges.

Just like the animal kingdom and humanity itself, religion evolves. Biological evolution occurs as new environmental challenges are overcome by living organisms. So, humanity and its religion evolved from an original condition—the contemporary condition. They will most likely evolve into something else in the future. Judaism is a great example of theo-evolution.

In the early years of Judaism, the people and priests would slaughter animals and offer them as burnt offerings to God. This was done in atonement of sins committed. However, though these procedures are written in detail in the Torah, we don't see it in practice today. Not one sect of Judaism continues the practice of animal sacrifice. Why? Because spiritual interpretation, social dynamic changes, and environmental demands caused changes in interpretation and application. Judaism, the human belief system, evolved just as humanity the organism did.

All religions can be plotted on a sort of family tree. Every one of them have root faiths or foundations and from there come different interpretations of the same general belief, adaptations, and the emergence of entirely new forms of belief. As we travel along the timeline the tree becomes broader and broader as new branches emerge from older ones and the older ones either continue on or stop entirely, allowing the newer branches and their branches to progress.

Where else is a tree like this seen? The evolution of species on earth is best viewed as a tree. It has roots, a trunk, and many branches from

Science and Religion

the trunk and branches from those branches. We can see how life relates and how it developed. Just as genetic changes bring about new but related organisms so too do the changes in belief and interpretation bring about newer but related human belief systems. As humans evolve so too does their religion and reasoning.

The Abrahamic Faiths

Abram was a man born in Ur many years before the Jewish prophets and thousands of years before the coming of Jesus Christ and Islam's Mohammad. Ur was a Mesopotamian city that is positioned in modern-day Iraq. He would later leave Ur with his family to a place known as Haran, located in modern-day Turkey.

It was here that Abram's father, Terah, passed away (Gen 11:32) and he received a divine command to leave Haran and go to a place he would be shown by God (12:1). He did as he was instructed and eventually ended up in Shechem of Canaan (12:4). This place is located just north of Bethel and Jerusalem in modern-day Israel.

Abram was promised by God that he would be the father of a great multitude and many nations (Gen 13:16, 15:5, and 17:5–6). Because he was to become the father of many he was renamed by God and called Abraham (17:5). The story doesn't end there, though. Abraham not only becomes the father of many nations but also of three great religions. These are Judaism, Christianity, and Islam.

All three major global religions claim their heritage to be in Abraham, the father of the multitudes and of many nations. All three faiths record the migratory story of Abram from Ur to Haran and on to Shechem. They go further to describe the births of Ishmael and Isaac (16:15, 17:21 and 21:2), the banishing of the eldest half-brother (21:14), and the near execution of the other (22:11) as a test to Abraham's faith and loyalty to God.

The story of Abraham is held as fact and spiritual truth by the teachings and Scriptures of Islam, Christianity, and Judaism. That joint belief and recognition is what allows them to be classified as Abrahamic religions. But, that is about all there is to their similarities.

Judaism

Judaism is among the world's oldest surviving religions. Its history goes back well over three thousand years. This religion, in a multitude of forms, has managed to remain in existence through some of the most tremendous disasters. Epidemics, exiles, and invasions are just a few of the disasters it has endured when others collapsed.

The term "Judaism" is a Latin-Greek term—with a twist of Anglicizing—that is further rooted in Hebrew. It is properly pronounced as "Judah-ism" while the more common pronunciations of "Ju-dae-ism" and "Ju-dee-ism" are improper. The Hebrew term for what we know as the land of Judah (the tribe of Judah, pronounced in English as "Joo-duh") is "Yehuda" (pronounced "Yeh-hoo-dah"). The Greeks and Romans translated this name into the closest form that existed in their languages. That would be Juda or Judah. However, in Latin it would sound more like "Yoo-dah."

Those who practice the Judaic faith and belong to its cultural grouping are known in English as Jews or being Jewish. These expressions are also plays on the Greco-Roman term of Judah. Basically, a person belonging to or practicing the Judaic faith is known as a "Ju" (pronounced "Jooh"). This is further developed and scripted in English to be "Jew." A person of Judaic origin or practice is known as "being Jewish." The labeling and title terms for this faith are really quite simple. This is especially so for English and many of the European languages because the Jewish community has been a part of these cultures for hundreds of years. This is also the same for the Mediterranean and Middle Eastern cultures.

A De-centralized and Factionalized Faith

Many people of various cultures and religions of the world, other than those that are Judaic or rooted in Judaism, tend to have some common and occasionally grotesque misconception of what Judaism is and what Jewish people are like. A primary misconception is that Judaism is completely united and whole in all of its ways, beliefs, workings, and manners. Nothing could be further from the truth.

This misunderstanding of Judaism was exploited by the Nazis. The German majority was convinced that the Jewish community was united and secretly plotting to eliminate the non-Jewish majority. Hitler seized on this and inflated the ignorance in order to control the masses through a

Science and Religion

common false-enemy. The reality is Judaism isn't and has never been that united.

The same, exploited misconception was used by the Soviet government under Joseph Stalin. His regime also told the masses, and justified their slaughtering of millions of innocent people, the false belief that all Jews were united to destroy non-Jews and they were capitalist abusers of the working class. He conveniently failed to mention that most of the working-class people were Jewish and the rich were mostly orthodox Christians. Neither Hitler nor Stalin would have been able to turn and control the majority population if the false perception of Jews plotting against the world wasn't already present in the minds of the common members of society at the time. They played on an already present bias that was under the stress of economic and political strain.

The sad truth is that Judaism's history is filled with arguments, violent clashes, banishing, and breakaway sect formation. In fact, contemporary Judaism has numerous sects that range from the traditional and conservative to New Age and liberal. Contemporary Judaism doesn't even remotely resemble the Judaism of the days when Abraham walked the earth. Even the most conservative contemporary sects of the Judaic belief system are nothing like the original Judaic root faith.

It is easy to see this, as in the earliest days of Judaism the priests and people performed and offered burnt animal sacrifices—and in one story nearly a human sacrifice—in atonement for their transgressions or to call upon God to look favorably upon them. These practices simply don't exist in modern Judaism but certainly did exist in the early days.

Even the priests of the great temple no longer exist. The priesthood, from the Levites, became obsolete and extinct when the temple was destroyed. There are only Rabbi's, or teachers, who teach, advise, and lead the faithful Jews of today. Judaism, like the social, technological, biological, and political elements of humanity, has evolved over time, from priests making animal sacrifices in the temple to the non-sacrificing and more philosophical rabbis in the synagogues of today.

Throughout the development history of Judaism there has not only been heated disagreement but violent rebellion and confrontation. In Exodus we find Moses came down from the mountain of Sinai and observed that some of the people had fashioned a golden calf and were worshipping it (Exod 32:19). It was a fall back to the Egyptian practices of their former masters (32:7–9). The result was the death of thousands of people (32:28).

What is Religion?

The calf was melted down, made into powder, then placed in water and poured down the throats of many (32:20).

This is but one of many documented incidents of disagreement and violent confrontation within the ranks of Judaism and throughout its history. Disagreement and division continues today, too. Happily, it hasn't been nearly as violent as it was in the early days. The misconception of unity and plotting comes from the experiences of outsiders who have encroached or even waged outright war against them.

Even though they argue and fuss within their own ranks, as any related group or family would do from time to time, they will quickly set aside these differences to face any threat or challenge offered by outside elements. Like brothers they will fuss, bicker, and even throw punches from time to time, but if somebody outside the family messes with any member of the family all internal conflict disappears and they all come down on the outside threat. This isn't a characteristic unique to Judaism, either. It is present in all forms of social groups along all points of the human-occupied timeline.

Transitional Judaism

To further understand Judaism one must examine its developmental roots and processes. This means one cannot fully understand and appreciate modern Judaism without understanding and appreciating historical Judaism. One has evolved from the other over time.

Many people tend to believe or interpret the Scriptures to mean the Jewish faith developed instantly by the decree of God. Some would assert Judaism started with the creation of Adam and Eve. Of course, this isn't held by all onlookers, whether they are part of or outside the faith. Others argue it is nothing greater than an invention of the human mind to explain away all things humans cannot understand at the time.

They, the ones who see religion as a non-spiritual and purely sociological organ, assert it was created in one form and morphed as humankind's needs and understanding of the surrounding environment changed. It evolved as humanity evolved, they say. The evolution of humans and their religion is an interesting point. But, is that all there is?

The reality is it is spiritual and documents the divine while changing as humanity changes. It is better to think of this, Judaism or otherwise, as something that is of the spirit but changes with the conditions of nature. It allows the spirit to adapt with the body to the ever-changing circumstances of nature while remaining connected to that which makes nature. Thus, nature and the divine define humanity and its place is between the two.

So, where are Judaism's beginnings? For this author it is quite clearly rooted in the divine. Unfortunately, it isn't the religion of Abraham that serves as the launch point for religion. There were many that existed before it. Uniquely, there is a piece of Judaism in every one of those earlier religions. Noah's flood can be correlated or related to the stories of Gilgamesh and so on.

In fact, the earliest roots of Judaism can't be concretely called monotheistic (a belief in only one God and nothing else) but rather monolatristic[1] (the worshipping of one God against other Gods). The adaptation of spiritual stories of ancient Samaria regarding the creation of the world and the great flood are perfect examples of how early Semitic culture developed from pre-existing cultural beliefs.

Two major elements believed to have originated in the combination of elements from other polytheistic traditions spring from the developmental perspective of Judaism. The first is known as Monolatric Judaism and the second is Monotheistic Judaism. There is not a sudden appearance of Judaism. That is so for every religion. Instead, there is a gradual development into true monotheism. Like baking a cake, there are ingredients taken from here and a few from there. But, the finished product comes after time and patience as it bakes and develops.

Not every scholar and religious leader agrees with or subscribes to the development concept of Judaism. It is a matter of faith and this is fine. But, the evidence is quite strong in support of a spiritual assimilation and later evolution into what is seen today.

The evidence supporting the religious development perspective is seen by comparing the early books of Genesis, Exodus, Numbers, and Deuteronomy (along with other sacred scripts) with the tablets and stories that originate in the preceding Samarian and other regional cultures. The similarities in practice and temple construction are also significant evidence-generating areas. Historians and archaeologists are discovering, almost daily, new things that further support the development of Judaic monotheism. Even Monotheistic Judaism has evolved over the millennia.

---

1. Dan Cohn-Sherbok, *Judaism: History, Belief, and Practice* (New York: Rutledge, 2003), 940.

Many examples of transition can be read in the Torah. It was the God of Israel not El of Canaan who created the world and universe. It was God not Baal who was the source of rain and agricultural success. The catch is both Baal and El are seen and spoken of as competing gods rather than absolute falsities or constructs of the imagination. They are not defined or addressed as fabrications at all in the early days. Basically, it was a case of "my God is bigger and better than yours." Only later would the writings and proclamations of Judaism assert only one true God and no others.

In the story of the creation of the world and of humanity, the story of Adam and Eve written in the book of Genesis, one discovers a rather unique and puzzling exclamation by God. It occurs when God discovers Adam and Eve ate the fruit of the tree of knowledge. "See! *The man has become like one of us*, knowing what is good and what is bad! Therefore, he must not be allowed to put out his hand to take fruit from the tree of life also, and thus eat it and live forever" (Gen 3:22, emphasis mine).

Who is God speaking to? He said "us." If there is but one God, then there is no "us," right? This is what would be presented in a fully developed monotheistic belief system. There simply is no *us*. In monolatristic belief there is one God superior to all others, but there are others. In this view there would be an "us." So, we have in the Scriptures evidence of monolatristicism. There is more, though.

We see the evidence for monolatristic belief in early Semitic culture in the story of the Garden of Eden. But, where does one find evidence of transition to monotheistic Judaism? There are many examples but one stands out as being among the earliest indicators of transition. This occurs in the book of Exodus and the story of Moses. In this story Moses is told by God to tell the people "I am" (3:14). This indicates God is and there is nothing else. Here, the transition from the greatest among the gods to the only God, the God of Israel can be seen.

Orthodox Judaism

Orthodox Judaism is said to be practiced in accordance with the original laws and traditions that date back as far as Abraham. The followers of this form of Judaism strive to live as closely to basic and original rules and traditions of the Torah as possible. They also adhere to the Talmudic texts and the oral traditions rendered by later Jewish scholars (Gaonim, Rishonim, Acharonim).

Science and Religion

According to the Jewish Federations of North America (JFNA), an approximate 13 percent of American Jews are of the Orthodox religious persuasion.[2] The number is even higher in Israel where 25 percent of the Jewish population is Orthodox.[3] The strongest populations of Orthodox Jews are seen in Israel, United States, and various European and Eurasian countries. But, they can be found in smaller groups in almost every nation around the globe.

Though it is often labeled and treated as traditional or of being of the early Judaic practices and beliefs, Orthodox Judaism is really quite modern and absent of many of the rituals and processes instituted during the early days of the Jewish faith. In fact, the Semitic practices of Abraham's day are practically non-existent today.

Judaism, be it Orthodox or otherwise, is often self-portrayed as being a tight federation of synagogues, but the reality is it is more of a confederation. There is no formal and absolute central authority or leadership. There are committees and various authoritative boards, but no supreme rabbi or temple priest who makes decrees and interpretations. There are arguing scholars and rabbis from one group to the next, and each synagogue maintains autonomy while being united by commonly held beliefs, rules, and traditions. They come together to debate, resolve, and even defend one another against threats of all forms (be it a social, political, financial, industrial, or military threat).

The fractionalization of Judaism goes well beyond the general differences of orthodox, conservative, and liberal faith. There are denominations within Orthodoxy such as Hasidism and the Mitnagdim. These subgroups exist solely because of interpretive and applicatory differences. Further, each synagogue is slightly different.

At first glance, one is left with the feeling that Judaism is on the brink of total dissolution because few of the leadership and scholars can manage to agree on anything. The glue is in the mentality of the Semitic people. Unlike other cultures, Jews can disagree without hatred and rejection. They can argue like cats and dogs but then come together like a family in times of crisis, celebration, and homage to God. It is both rare and wonderful as most cultures split violently and hatefully from unresolved dispute. But,

---

2. "Report Series on the National Jewish Population Survey 10." In *American Jewish Religious Denominations* (New York: United Jewish Communities, 2005), 9.

3. Ibid., 5.

these people can maintain a position and argue that position passionately without losing their identity and unity.

Hasidic orthodoxy was founded by Ba'al Shem Tov in the eighteenth century. Since its founding Hasidism has expanded exponentially and can be found in all parts of the world today. Its largest concentrations exist in Israel, Europe, and North America. Hasidics are distinguished by locks of hair and traditional dark clothes and hats.

Hasidism focuses primarily on a sincere and intense prayer inclusive of spiritually charged dancing and singing. This allows the followers of Hasidism to commune or connect better with God. There is also a strict adherence to the old ways of the Tanakh. Within Hasidic Judaism exists several subgroups such as the Chabad, Lubavitch, Belzer, Satmar, and Breslav. These groups came into existence following the death of Ba'al Shem Tov.

Mitnagdimic orthodoxy started when disputes erupted regarding interpretation and practice. The term "Mitnagdim" translates to mean "the opponents." Their argument is that while anyone could practice the sincere and simple approach of Hasidism only an ascetic, academic, and serious study of Talmud and Torah can be permitted. Put more directly, absolute focus on the teachings and traditions must be in place and only a select few are qualified to study and express interpretation. This, then, makes Mitnagdimism the most central lead form of Judaism.

Many practitioners of Orthodox Judaism can be easily identified because they wear the traditional, eighteenth-century dark clothes and hats. These people are also distinguished by the long curly locks of hair along the sides of their faces and the long beards. However, not all Hasidics wear the traditional garb. Some have even taken to wearing modern yet conservative fashion. Blue jeans and T-shirts are common and popular among today's youth.

Conservative Judaism

Although this form of Judaism is labeled conservative, it is really the moderate form. In fact, it is also known as "goldilocks Judaism." Just as the story implies, conservative Judaism is not too hot or too cold, but just right in the middle. It isn't as strict as Orthodoxy, but isn't as loose as liberal Judaism. Of course, to the orthodox they aren't practicing Judaism but something else.

Science and Religion

Conservative Judaism started in the nineteenth century as many Jews began to believe the Reform movement went too far in shedding certain traditions and interpretations of spiritual law. However, they still saw Orthodoxy as archaic and too strict. In essence, the Orthodox Jews were seen as unrealistic and the Reformers were seen as too distant. So, they formed their own synagogues and embraced what they believed should be kept and rejected what was seen as no longer applicable to the faith.

This moderate Judaic movement was the largest group in the United Kingdom and the United States. However, their numbers have begun to decline as more and more members find themselves drawn to reformist and orthodox synagogues. This exodus from conservative Judaism is credited mainly to the decision to allow women to be ordained as rabbis within conservative Judaism. It is easy to see where the truly conservative were offended by a break from tradition and the liberal were repulsed by open objection to change.

Reformist Judaism

Reform Judaism is probably the largest group in the United States and Canada. Its core belief is that all Jews have the responsibility and obligation to educate themselves and make decisions about their own individual spiritual practice. It is important to apply the holy texts and teachings to contemporary times. They do not see the Scriptures as coming directly from God, but as inspired by God. Therefore, they were written by men in their era and what is today makes those interpretations irrelevant and inapplicable. It is important to re-evaluate the Torah, Tanakh, and Talmud in order to find better meaning in them for the Jews of today.

Rules and traditions seen as archaic and inhibitive of modern Jews have been stripped away in Reform Judaism. They strip away what is recognized as unessential and try to stick with the core of Jewish belief and faith. This has left the rest of the Jewish community with the perspective that Reformism is a group of people with empty and meaningless services. They have even been critically described as wanting to retain the label of Jew while participating in none of its traditions, beliefs, and practices. The truth of that remains in the eye of the beholder, though.

There are some significant differences, though. One is that the Reformists Jews began to seat women and men together during services. Another is the practical elimination of the dietary laws of Judaism. That alone is seen as a complete rift from Judaism by those of the conservative and Orthodox Judaic persuasions. Additionally, women have been ordained as rabbis in the reformist movement. Although conservative Jews also ordain women, Orthodox Jews see this as an absolute offense to the faith and God.

The uniqueness of this movement is its size and growth rate. Unlike other cultural liberal movements that tend to consist of a small minority of fringe people trying to pick at the mainstream elements of their culture for change, Reform Judaism is large and growing. It can be very easily determined as the largest Jewish movement in North America. So, one is left wondering if Reform Judaism is North America's mainstream Judaism, opposed to the more traditional and aged Orthodox and conservative Jewish movements.

Reconstructionist Judaism

Reconstructionism has its roots in the seventeenth century when a philosopher named Baruch Spinoza declared God was no entity per se, but rather the accumulated/combined forces of nature. This did not go well within the Jewish community of the time and he was denounced and excommunicated. All Jews were told they were not to read or even touch Spinoza's written works or to listen to his orations.

Although the consequences of this revelation were considerably severe for Spinoza, he planted a seed in the hearts and minds of many young Jews of the time. They would secretly explore this concept and eventually become seniors and rabbis themselves. With time, Spinoza's work became commonplace in Jewish academia. But, it wasn't Spinoza alone.

Approximately three hundred years after Spinoza another theologian added to what would become reconstructionist Judaism. His name was Mordecai Kaplan. He also came to realize the same thing as Spinoza and published a prayer book that reflected this view of God. As with Spinoza, the Orthodox Jews burned his book, banned it, and excommunicated him. But this time it was only within the ranks of orthodoxy and not among other groups. Thus, there was a crack in the rock where the seed was able to grow into a seedling.

Kaplan was a conservative rabbi who taught at the Conservative Rabbinical Seminary. While there, he taught that God was not a being, but rather the totality of natural and moral forces that comprise the universe. Further, he went on to say every Jewish generation had an obligation to maintain Judaism by reconstructing it rather than stripping it down or adhering to archaic applications of Torah and Talmud. In others words, don't reject but re-interpret in accordance with the challenges and conditions of contemporary Jewish times. What was written meant one thing then but means something entirely different today.

Messianic Judaism

Messianic Judaism is the most interesting and perplexing belief system for theologians of the Christian persuasion. This is because in Messianism Jesus Christ is recognized as the Messiah of prophecy. They also believe he will come again someday in the future. This is no different than what Christians believe. Yet, they continue to practice the old Jewish traditions and laws.

Messianists are generally not accepted as being Jewish by the general Judaic population. They aren't what modern Christians would define as Christian, either. Their beliefs and traditions make them subject to rejection and criticism from other Jewish sects while simultaneously Christians see this as an acceptable, yet odd, form of Abrahamic belief. They have even been nicknamed "Jews for Jesus."

On the surface, Messianic Judaism appears to be some sort of hybrid form of Christianity. Some would even ask how they can continue to call themselves Jewish while proclaiming Jesus as the Messiah of Jewish prophecy. But, on deeper examination we see Jesus is a unique character among several Judaic sects. While some Jews reject Jesus as a falsity or insane character, others more commonly see him as a prophet or wise man.

Although the Jewish community at large has rather severe objection to this sect's beliefs and assertions, Christianity has been more accepting and in many cases feels as though Christ has been vindicated. For Christians this isn't hard to accept because in the time of Jesus and the apostles there was no term, "Christian." Christ was a Jew and his followers were Jews. One could even say the Jewish followers of Jesus were, "Jews for Jesus."

Christianity

In the beginning, Christianity was not known by a Christ-related name. There simply was no "Christianity" to mention or experience then. A Jew by the name of Jesus was born in Bethlehem, taken into Egypt, and later

What is Religion?

raised in Nazareth. He is said to have been the Son of God and performed many miracles, healings, and signs. Jesus had many followers with twelve, maybe thirteen, core followers known as apostles. He is recorded as having traveled throughout Israel in order to proclaim the good news, known as the gospel, to the people and to perform signs and miracles that softened the hearts of non-believers and converted the wayward. But, he and his followers weren't called Christians. They were called probably every derogatory term available at the time, but certainly not Christian.

Jesus and his followers were all Jews. They most likely originated from Pharisaical rather than Seducitic Judaism because of their social and economic status in the community. Either he was accepted as a prophet, the Son of God, or the Messiah or he was rejected and seen as a heretic or insane person. But, he and his followers were Jewish. Not unlike what we see in modern Messianic Judaism.

Jesus was proclaimed by his followers to be the Anointed One. In Hebrew this is known as Messiah and in Greek this is known as *khristos*. It is from the Greek word *khristos* we get the English term, "Christ." All three terms, "Jesus Christ," "Jesus the Messiah," and "Jesu Christos," mean the exact same thing: Jesus the Anointed. Naturally, to be a follower of Christ and his teachings is to be a Christian.

Many people believe the word "Christ," or Greek *khristos*, means to be the Son of God but this is incorrect and has never meant that. *Ios tu theus* is the Greek equivalent for the Son of God. In Greek written biblical texts and other documents on Christian divinity we see *ios* or *gios* used to represent the Son of God.

It wasn't until many years after the ascension of Jesus that people began to differentiate the Jews who followed Jesus from those who did not. Additionally, these Christian Jews were open to the conversion of non-Jewish people (the Gentiles). With time, it was simply shortened to the term "Christian" and all ties to the traditional Judaic faith broke as new customs and beliefs solidified among the followers of Jesus Christ. Christianity was a steady and rapid developmental process that started with Jesus and his apostles. It continued to evolve into the considerably diverse and global faith we see today.

Christianity, like the other Abrahamic faiths, is not a single, united faith in Jesus Christ. Indeed, it is fragmented and broken down into a plethora of denominations. In fact, Christianity has so many denominations that they could not possibly be covered in their entirety by this work. To be

Christian is one thing, but to be Catholic, Orthodox, Baptist, or Evangelical is another. However, they are all Christian because of the general beliefs that they hold. These beliefs are:

1. Jesus was born of a virgin in Bethlehem.
2. Jesus is the Son of God.
3. Jesus died on the cross in atonement for the sins of all humanity.
4. Jesus died, was buried, and descended into hell.
5. Jesus rose from the dead in three days.
6. Jesus stayed with the apostles for forty days and instructed them.
7. Jesus ascended into heaven and is seated at God's right hand.
8. Jesus will come again to judge all, living and dead.

Although the aforementioned core beliefs are held throughout Christendom, there are and have been many disagreements and differences in biblical interpretation and application. These more specific beliefs and definitions to scriptural purpose is what have led to a history of violent clashes and schismatic disagreement. Christians are a lot like their Judaic cousins in that they see God and his word from different perspectives and passionately argue their positions and views. Sometimes, more often than not, they argue and disagree to a point of impasse. This then leads to the establishment of new Christian sects/denominations. Unfortunately, these differences can often lead to violent conflict—even war. Roman Catholics have persecuted different assertions and the people who hold or propose them for centuries and have even fought bloody wars against Protestant led governments. In turn, Protestants have attacked and killed Catholics and radicals (e.g., Anabaptists) fought both Catholics and Protestants. What is the source of this horrid and needless violence?

If they are all Christian why do so much harm to one another? How can anyone call themselves Christian when they take up the sword against their own kin? It seems that Christianity would be even more powerful, influential, and productive if it were united. That is a very true statement but it simply isn't united. It is the answer to this question that has made purpose for this book. The answer is simple but the consequence is dire for all involved. It is not the religion. It is not the eight general principles of Christian belief or the stories recorded in the Holy Bible that divides but rather the rigidity and free choice of humanity.

Christian humanity, indeed all of humanity, finds itself bogged down in the interpretations and interpolations of the specifics of scripture and loses focus of the commonalities it has from one person to another. Humanity is stubborn and stiff necked. It tends to be rigid in its thoughts, practices, ideas, identities, and social definitives. So stubborn is the human race that it will resort to violence and mayhem before attempting to negotiate or to simply acknowledge an impasse and move on peacefully. Perhaps there is some natural desire, an animal characteristic, within us all that drives us to assert our beliefs and desires upon others. Is there a drive for dominance, maybe?

When the Christian bible is objectively read one discovers that there is only one absolute. That God loves humanity and humanity is designed to want a relationship with Him. All other things therein and thereafter are matters of time, space, and perspective. What is seen today won't be there tomorrow and where it is seen from one point it is not from another. This is the wonder of the Holy Scriptures and the greatness of God. The bible, the scriptures, and prophets have been divine gifts to humankind. They are a source for unity and love for one another not strife and division. It is humanity and its rigidity, stubbornness, and uncontrolled desire for dominance that has led to war and division and not the principles of faith or God.

Early Christendom

Christianity came into its own in the later part of the first century. This is when it was being labeled at-large as Christian rather than Jewish. The term is said by many historians to have been an insult by those who used it. But, much of Christianity, especially in terms of doctrine and creed, was yet to be developed. The full Christian identity would come in to being during the fourth century with the Nicene councils. But, it was rocky even then as bishops and patriarchs of the post-apostolic period would disagree and argue from one end of the Christian world to the other.

Many of the bishops plotted against one another and used political and spiritual influence to denounce, oust, and even execute bishops and clerics with opposing religious views. The bishops in Rome asserted they were the successors to Peter and should thus be the leaders of all Christendom. The eastern and north African churches asserted that either Constantinople should be the lead office or each bishop, representing a different apostle, should act equal to the others and general doctrine and dogma should be the result of a council process.

Early disagreements centered on the admission of Gentiles and whether or not they should first follow Jewish dietary rules and become circumcised. Other disagreements were over the exact birth date of Jesus. Of course, the struggle for absolute power and influence over all other churches and bishops was ever present in these times. It is, after all, an inseparable part of humanity's darker side.

After Jesus ascended into heaven the apostles were left to carry on the message and to spread the word and faith throughout the world and to all nations. The apostles worked to spread the faith throughout the Mediterranean, Egypt, Syria, Assyria, and further east. Peter went to Rome; Paul traveled throughout modern-day Turkey, Macedonia, and Greece; Andrew went and worked to establish belief in Palestine; Bartholomew went on to Armenia; and Thomas is believed by many to have made it as far as modern-day Pakistan. This period is known as the apostolic Christian period.

In regards to the asserted belief that Thomas went eastward, reaching as far as Pakistan, one sees through examination of another religion there is strong evidence suggesting he was indeed there. Aside from the fact there are Christians in the area who acknowledge this in modern times and recorded his presence and preaching during the apostolic Christian period, there is a sect of Islam that also recognizes his presence and sees him as a prophet.

This Islamic sect is known as Ahmadiyya Islam and it sees Thomas not as an apostle who taught in the area, but as Jesus Christ. This strain of Islam asserts that Jesus survived the cross and went on to preach in Pakistan. They acknowledge him as the Messiah. They hold him in high regard and even believe he has already returned through the Ahmadiyya founder. Additionally, they claim Jesus died of natural causes in advanced age somewhere in the Kashmir region.

Thomas the apostle is known today as St. Thomas the apostle, but had several other names. One was "doubting Thomas" because of his reaction to the initial reports of Jesus's resurrection. But, there was another name he was known by, too. That name was "Thomas the Twin" because of his remarkable likeness to Jesus of Nazareth. Could this be a source of confusion that would lead Ahmadiyya Muslims to believe it was actually Christ? Who knows? But, the circumstances certainly do raise eyebrows in curiosity and wonder for most that learn of it.

What is Religion?

The post-apostolic Christian period is roughly defined as starting in the second century and lasting all the way through to its official recognition by Emperor Constantine. The term "post-apostolic" simply identifies the period when successor bishops to the apostles controlled early church doctrine and philosophy. When the last apostle to Christ died the post-apostolic era began. It was during this period, like that of the apostolic period, that Christianity was under constant persecution and many Christians were tortured and executed gruesomely. Many of the early martyr saints came to be during this period. This is especially so in Rome.

Secrecy and survival were the primary issues on every Christian's mind. Services were held in secret and gatherings occurred in obscure places—usually in caves or abandoned mines, even catacombs. A great example can be seen in Salzburg, Austria where a church was built into a catacomb and services were held secretly to avoid persecution and even execution. This church still exists today and can be toured as the Salzburg Catacombs. At the top of the mountain is a monastery. In Rome, the catacombs were also used for secret Christian gatherings. Beyond that, believers would gather to celebrate and worship in their homes.

It was too self-destructive to plot and provoke intrigue between leaders with different views and biblical interpretations. Plus, many of the early leaders knew Christ personally and understood well what was meant by his preaching and teaching. There were too few of the faithful and too many enemies to allow for open strife anyway. This is not to say disagreement in interpretation and biblical application did not exist, but rather that the arguments remained mild and friendly in order to prevent exposure to foes intent on their absolute destruction.

It wasn't until after Emperor Constantine officially recognized Christianity and made it a state religion that Christians could relax a bit. Of course, this brought the church into the intrigues and politics of the imperial court and the result was a dark and divisive time for Christendom. Those dark impacts would ring through to the present day. Bishops of the religion sprang into new political, social, and economic status and this soon tempted man's darker side to arise.

There were bishops in Jerusalem, Alexandria, Rome, Damascus, Caesarea, Carthage, Constantinople, and so on. Each bishop rooted his position and authority in one apostle or another. For instance, in Rome the bishops claimed to be the direct successors of the Apostle Peter. Paul was claimed in the East and so on. Arguments erupted over practice, interpretation, mass, history, and leadership. Unfortunately, many used political and social influence to have other bishops removed via execution or assassination.

During the Nicene period of early Christendom the bishops and priestly scholars of the time were absent of the personal experience—the physical experience—of Jesus Christ. This is in stark contrast with the apostles who knew him personally. Many of the bishops were from royal or wealthy families and did not share the same perspective as Christ; few followed his humble and poverty-ripe way of life and prayer. They were, however, quite familiar with the politics of empire, wealth, and society.

Thus, where a person cannot be dominated, dictated to, or convinced to agree by another he or she becomes a foe rather than a friend in kind disagreement or individuality. Unlike the apostles who could disagree and even rebuke one another without succumbing to hatred and ill will, these successors were different. The bishop of Rome, later to be called Pope (Latin for "father"), asserted he was the successor to Peter and it was Peter who Jesus said was the rock upon which his church would be built. They argued this was an appointment of Peter over all other apostles, and thus all successor bishops should be led by the bishop of Rome. This certainly was not taken well by the bishops in Alexandria, Jerusalem, Constantinople, and Antioch. A struggle for dominance and power quickly developed.

Unfortunately, though the church grows in this period and reaches recognition and imperial protection, its leadership became no better than the typical courtiers and aristocrats of the pagan empire. In fact, many were drawn from the ranks of the nobility and aristocracy. It was common practice for the youngest sons of noble and royal families to be placed in the church as priests and monks. These were people who were raised as generals and political leaders. They were, by nature, ambitious. Such a predisposition makes piousness difficult at best.

It is interesting to note that shortly after Christianity entered into the Nicene period the type of people who entered the leadership were seldom of humble beginnings. The style and expense of churches, altars, and holy items became gold encrusted and extravagant. Priests and bishops began to wear expensive and flashy garments. It would appear these new leaders were too attached to the material world to continue the humble ways of Christ and his apostles.

These leaders were also greatly involved in court politics and social manipulation. They were both manipulated by and used the politicians and powers of governance and faith to achieve personal goals and political ambitions. It was difficult for them to let go of that and the result was horrid arguing, rigidity, and even murderous efforts.

Would any of us see Jesus Christ wearing expensive garments, dwelling in a home of gold and silver, jumping into political intrigue, or placing his pride and ego before God and his people? Would he have struck Thomas down for doubting or did he slay Judas for his treachery? Certainly not, yet the early Christian leaders of the Nicene period did all these things. They did what Jesus detested of the Sadducees. We watch the holy mass in celebration of Christ's last meal; the priest sips from a golden chalice while Christ got a commoner's cup. Certainly, these doings of the noble priesthood are not in keeping with Christ or the religion, but rather the greed and decadence of the individual in the position.

Even today, we see our reverend brothers and sisters falling for the lure of luxury and gold when evangelists live in twelve-million-dollar homes, ride in expensive cars, eat the finest foods, and wear the finest clothes while their congregations give when they have little and eat what they can get when they can get it. We see the Pope and patriarchs living in super mansions, partaking in the world's politics, flying in private jets, and wearing $20,000 garments. The chalices used in the mass of many Roman and Orthodox cathedrals cost between $10,000 and $15,000 each. What was the cost of our Lord's cup?

Is this what Christ taught? Is that how he lived? Is this what he meant by living well and righteous? Should we all admire this or shake the dust from our sandals as we walk away? Is this the religion or the greed of men? It is certainly something we should all think about the next time we are saying amen before accepting the body and blood of Christ.

Needless to say, the absence of the apostles and the introduction and dominance of faith by the aristocratic and royal led the church away from the basic foundations of Christian belief and practice. The humbleness and connection with the common person slowly decayed and was replaced by extravagant shows in the mass, clerical dress, and even arrogance among the monastics. Later, this degeneration among the elements of divine servitude would lead to great and bloody wars against other Christians, Jews, and Muslims.

They, the Christian leadership, seem to have moved away from service to God and others and the acceptance of free will and willful conversion to a concept of Christianity by the sword, with a very narrow definition of what is Christian. Those who review this part of Christian history are forced to ask whether this transition was divine or strictly human. Was this transition a divine intervention or the ignorance, greed, and ambitions of men?

The Church of Rome

The Church of Rome, more commonly known today as the Roman Catholic Church, existed at the same time as the eastern churches. However, this part of early Christendom had significant differences with the others, and this came to a head in 1054 C.E. when Cardinal Humbert, acting on behalf of Pope Leo IX, demanded that the patriarch Cerularius of Constantinople acknowledge the supremacy of Rome and its bishop (Pope). He then refused Cerularius recognition as a patriarch. Needless to say, this didn't go over well with Cerularius and he flatly refused the invitation to be subjugated by Rome.

Of course, the patriarch's refusal wasn't received well either. In retaliation, Cardinal Humbert issued a decree of excommunication against Cerularius. This then led to a retaliatory excommunication from the patriarch against the Cardinal. It has been widely believed that Pope Leo IX and Patriarch Cerularius excommunicated one another. But this is inaccurate as Pope Leo IX died while Cardinal Humbert was negotiating with the Eastern Church leadership, and the patriarch's excommunication decree dealt only with Humbert and his accompanying legates.

The whole argument was like an elementary school playground dispute. It is sort of like two big kids in the park saying:
"You better join our club and follow me!"
"I'll not! Your club stinks!"
"Oh yeah?"
"Yeah?"
"Well then, you can never join our club. You are out!"
"Fine I'll stick with my own mates here and you can never join our club!"
"Fine!"
"Fine. Humf!" And they part.

What would be known as the Great Schism came to be in about the same manner. From that point on we have an irreconcilable difference that created the Eastern Orthodox Church and the Roman Catholic Church (the church of Rome). Each will dominate their geographical regions

What is Religion?

respectively and go on to evangelize many other places in competition with one another. Just like two schoolyard gangs, each church's leadership would accuse the other of starting the fight and being bullies. It is amazing how childlike adults can become at times.

This seems to be another one of those areas in history where the author has an opportunity to ask his question. Is this the doing of God and the consequence of holy Scripture or the doings of men with great ambition? Did God or Jesus tell Pope Leo IX to go forth and subdue the leaders of the eastern churches? Do the Scriptures say the Pope or Peter is the dominant leader of all Christendom? No, these disputes and division came from the interpretation men put upon the Scriptures and the assumption—or rather misrepresentation—they were acting for God. This split isn't by the order or will of God, but by the ambitious, power-craving, and covetous nature of humankind.

From this great split (or schism) was born the Roman Catholic Church. Based in Rome, it has managed to dominate social, spiritual, financial, and political affairs in Western Europe and other places around the world for hundreds of years. It has instigated and led world wars, and it has been the justification for many a tyrant. But, in the same breath it has housed the homeless, given growth space to science, built libraries, advanced mathematics, developed the concept of public education, raised the bar on morality, and given hope to the hopeless. It gives a sense of purpose where all other manner of study and meditation fail to do so.

So what is Roman Catholicism? What makes it unique from all other forms of Christianity? It has a history in common with other Christian sects such as the Orthodox Christian and Coptic Christian churches. But, following the Great Schism it developed its own identity, practices, and beliefs.

In order to call oneself Roman Catholic there are a number of beliefs and practices that must be adopted and a process that must be undertaken. To understand this very large and complex form of Christianity the observer must start with its beliefs. There are five general principles of belief held by the Church of Rome and shared by its followers. These are:

1. The Bible is a collection of holy written works that were written by men but inspired by God. It is believed the canonized Bible of the Catholic Church is free of any errors or blemishes. The Bible is the ultimate written authority.

2. Baptism, a ritual cleansing of body and soul with water, is necessary for salvation. Baptism can occur through water, blood, or desire.
3. The Ten Commandments are the primary moral and ethical rules by which all of humanity should live and act.
4. The concept of the Holy Trinity. This is among the more complicated beliefs and declarations of the Roman Church. Indeed, other Christian denominations adopt this perspective as well. The Trinity concept is a form of viewing Jesus Christ as the Son of God, God as the Father Almighty, and the Holy Spirit as the will and power of God. In Roman Catholicism these three beings represent a totality of one all-powerful, all-knowing, and loving God.

There is a special view of the human body and soul this denomination holds. What makes it interesting is it seems more in common with contemporary science, at least is highly compatible, than what is often portrayed by critics in the media and scientific community. Roman Catholicism recognizes the unity of body and soul for each and every human being now, before, and beyond. Humanity is unique in it exists in both the natural and spiritual worlds simultaneously. The physical world, like that of the spirit, is considered a creation of God and is inherently good until misused by an individual or group.

This is interesting as science says a very similar thing. With the exception of divine action it agrees the natural world started somewhere, and that it is balanced and good until recklessly tampered with by humanity. All can agree the universe has its rules and means of harmonious existence that can turn terribly violent and disastrous when they are meddled with.

There is an incredible amount of similarity between science and religion from the Catholic Christian perspective. Many scientists will openly say the only reason scientific journals, articles, and reports do not include divinity is that physical evidence of the existence and intervention of and by the divine cannot be established. Just like many priests and theologians will say a physical search for the divine is futile and thus the requirement for faith.

Catholic Christians go through a special process and participate in certain rituals that fully indoctrinate, cleanse, and accept them as children and followers of Jesus Christ and the Holy Father, God—the creator of all. Every person must undergo these processes and rituals in order to be considered fully Christian.

What is Religion?

Among these rites and processes are what have come to be labeled as sacraments. A sacrament is a ritual or tradition instituted by Jesus Christ personally. There are seven sacraments: baptism, penance, Eucharist (or communion), confirmation, matrimony, holy orders, and the anointing of the sick. Each sacrament represents a significant step in the development of the human spirit in teachings of Jesus.

Contrary to popular perception, the church of Rome and the concepts and community of science are not at odds. In fact, the church has made it quite clear that theology and science walk hand-in-hand, as one explores and defines the mechanics and means of the physical world and the other explains the issues of spirituality and human purpose.

The Orthodox Christian Churches

Christian Orthodoxy is the more conservative and traditional following of Jesus's teachings and decrees. Just as Orthodox Judaism is the keeper of the old ways for the Jewish community, so too is Orthodox Christianity the keeper of the old ways of Christendom. The early Christian church was not divided along labels of Orthodox and Roman Catholicism. This would develop in the Nicene era of Christian history.

The Great Schism of 1054 C.E. would usher in the labels of Orthodox and Roman Catholic Christianity as each side sought to distinguish and distance themselves from each other. A general observation of Orthodox Christianity reveals that it holds almost identical theological views as those of the church of Rome. The biggest difference is how the leadership chain is developed and maintained within Orthodoxy. Other differences include the marriage of clerics, use of leavened vs. unleavened bread during communion, iconography in worship, and the order of the mass.

The leadership chain of the various Orthodox Christian churches is distinctively different than that of the related Roman Catholic Church. Unlike Romanism, Orthodox Christianity does not have a strong, centralized command and control element. Each region has its own bishop and these lesser bishops are led by regional patriarchs. Each patriarchy is independent of the others but joined through common belief and interaction. Thus, the Orthodox Christian faith is a sort of confederate system comprised of equal and independent bishoprics. The result is the development of the Russian Orthodox, Ethiopian Orthodox, Greek Orthodox, Jerusalem Orthodox, and many other churches (including those for the United States

Science and Religion

and Great Britain). There are agreements, conclaves, summits, and councils throughout its history that have produced the general beliefs of Orthodox Christianity, while there are slightly different and unique practices from patriarchy to patriarchy.

Orthodox Christianity is foreign to many in the western hemisphere where Protestant churches and Roman churches with Catholic origins prevail. Because this particular faith is rich in tradition and ritual it is often viewed as archaic and backward. However, such thinking is terribly erroneous. Like its Roman relative, Orthodox Christianity does not object to or attempt to suppress science, scientists, or the discoveries made. Instead, they embrace science as the means by which humanity discovers the revealing of the divine in the mechanics of the physical world. Science is not viewed as bad, but rather it is viewed as good and gifted to humanity by God.

Where strong arguments and objections come into play one finds it isn't the science but rather the misuse and abuse of its discoveries by individuals or groups. Such abuses lead to immoral acts and nature-destroying conditions that are seen by the religious as an attack on God and his holy order. These objections and moral applications of Orthodox Christianity are mirrored in the general code of ethics followed by the scientific community at large. Thus, they are not and have never been opposites or opponents, but rather two parts of a greater whole in understanding the universe and humanity's place and purpose in it.

There are some issues regarding the theory of human evolution and the belief in creationism. In fact, it is quite heated when the topic comes up. On one hand, there are scientists who say there is significant evidence to support the belief that humankind evolved from lesser creatures over time. On the other hand are those who believe humankind and all other life on earth were spontaneously created at the command of God. The accusations and condemnations, however, come solely from the more stubborn and radicalized elements of each side. The average person in the middle contemplates the two beliefs but goes on without decision, judgment, or strife. He or she simply waits until more information is discovered or revealed.

Regardless, this is a debate of two opposing theories and not an argument over whether science is good or religion is obsolete. The theory of evolution is heavily debated within the ranks of the scientific community itself. Of course, there are those among the religious who assert God worked over time and evolution was just the process of creating perfection. The battle lines aren't drawn along science and religion, but between people

What is Religion?

who see, experience, and exist in both. The bottom line is that what is believed regarding evolution and creationism is entirely up to the individual.

Protestantism

Today, the term "Protestant" is basically used to describe any Christian church that is not a part of the Roman Catholic, Eastern Orthodox, or Asian Orthodox churches. However, the term was much more specific in its beginnings. Then, a protestant movement was related specifically to reformist churches that sprang-up in Germany, England, Switzerland, and Scandinavia.

The word "protestant" is derived from the Latin term *protestari*, which means to speak against or protest. The word was applied to reformers, reformist movements, and reformed churches after German princes, of Lutheran leanings, signed a protest document, known as the Protestantium, in 1529. This was issued in objection to the Diet of Speyer that reaffirmed the banning of Martin Luther's *Ninety-Five Theses* by the Diet of Worms in 1521.

A German monk and priest by the name of Martin Luther observed certain practices within the church of Rome that were counter to the teachings of Christ, biblically unfounded, and occasionally fraudulent. His biggest issue was with the selling of indulgences to the laity in order for the Vatican to finance expensive building projects in Rome. He wasn't necessarily against indulgences, but he was against selling them because it was equivalent to a person buying his or her way into heaven. There were other abuses that, in Martin Luther's eyes, were in need of desperate reformation.

Luther was a monk of many years who struggled with purity and monastic principles, and whose constant penance and introspection gained the attention of the abbot. He was ordered to pursue an academic career in order to relieve his obsessive self-evaluation. He would serve as a priest and professor of theology at Wittenberg University in 1508.

At the same time Luther was entering professorship, Pope Leo X and his staff of cardinals and bishops were pursuing an ambitious and expensive building campaign in Rome that quite nearly drained the general coffers dry while leaving the Pope's budget free of affect. The answer to bankruptcy and the use of papal funding was to sell indulgences and exploit holy relics for as much as could be acquired. In short, the Vatican conspired and

35

hatched a racket to finance their desire for luxury seen not even by the kings of the day.

In 1516, a Dominican friar, Johann Tetzel, was sent to Germany by the Vatican to sell indulgences. Luther was appalled by this, as his argument was grace alone (*sola gratia*) saves the sinful and one cannot buy his or her way into heaven. But, the friar argued that belief alone does not make a saved person. Instead, Friar Johann asserted faith must be accompanied by charity and good works (*fides caritate formata*). Regardless of the theological argument, giving indulgences in exchange for money was the goal of the Vatican at the time.

Martin Luther, on October 31, 1517, wrote to his bishop, Albert of Mainz, to protest the sale of indulgences. This letter was accompanied by another document entitled "Disputation of Martin Luther on the Power and Efficacy of Indulgences." That document would be later known by the more easily recognized *Ninety-Five Theses*. Number eighty-six was seen by the bishop and the rest of church leadership as a direct challenge to the Pope. It read, "Why does the Pope, whose wealth today is greater than the wealth of the greatest Crassus, build the basilica of St. Peter with the money of poor believers rather than with his own money?"

Although it has been taught in many history classes over many years that Martin Luther posted his ninety-five theses on the door of the All Saints' Church in Wittenberg, Germany, there is very little evidence to support this. The story is believed to have originated with Phillip Malanchthon. However, there is strong evidence that suggests Phillip was not present to personally witness the alleged event.[4] The personality and ways of doing business for Martin Luther would seem to indicate an improbability of bringing his objections to the public immediately.

It is more likely Martin sent his ninety-five theses to the bishop and from there the inflammation within the church leadership grew. The bishop needed the funds of indulgence sales in order to finance his diocese, and the Pope was to receive half of the revenue to build the basilica of St. Peter in Rome. Thus, it is entirely plausible for one to conclude that the bishop was clouded by worldly financial matters and was not as concerned for accuracy in obedience to the divine as he should have been. To agree or acknowledge what was submitted to him by Martin would mean a confession of his own

---

4. Henrick Bekker. *Dresden, Leipzig, and Saxony Adventure Guide* (Oxford: Hunter Publishing, 2010), 125.

waywardness. The document received no response but was instead sent to the Vatican to be reviewed for heresy.

Luther was immediately ordered to retract his theses and challenges to papal leadership, to which he refused and prepared to argue his case. Martin Luther took a Papal bull issued against him—which demanded he recant his statements or face excommunication—and burned it publicly. This is when he started his most public and political push against the wrongful ways of the church. Naturally, this led to his being excommunicated on December 10, 1520.

Starting on January 28, 1521 and ending on May 25, 1521 the Diet of Worms convened to discuss the Reformist challenge. Martin Luther was ordered to appear before the panel and did so on April 18, 1521. He was well prepared and argued his position diligently and effectively. Of course, nothing was resolved between the two sides of the dispute and at the conclusion a ban on Martin Luther's *Ninety-Five Theses* and other writings was issued.

Many of the principalities and kingdoms of the holy Roman Empire and other related states supported Martin Luther's position and refused to arrest or have him executed for heresy. In fact, the princes of these states would come together and sign the "Protestantium," which would later be the basis for the movement's new name: Protestants.

There were other outspoken leaders of the Reformist Movement, too. There were the many writers and speakers of the Anabaptists, John Calvin and the Calvinist movement, and the Anglicans of Great Britain. Though there were differences in doctrine and interpretation by and between these movements, their general beliefs and objections to the doings of the Roman Church were the same. To a significant degree, these shared beliefs rendered strong social, religious, and political unity.

Since the church of Rome had significant resources and political control it maneuvered to crush reformism. However, the reformists were quickly gaining converts, financial support, and political backing. In fact, it was more the politics behind the religious perspectives that were at odds, more so than the religious issues. As was the case for virtually every war, politicians seized on the western Christian Schism to justify waging warfare against other kingdoms and states. The true goal was to satisfy their desire to expand their political control and wealth, but the publicly stated goal was to either reform Christianity or eliminate heresy depending on whose side they were on.

Science and Religion

Soon, there was much fighting. Warfare broke out all over central Europe with kings and princes drawing lines along the principles of Christian philosophy and interpretation. Again, the reality was purely political and rooted in military ambition. In order for the poor of any nation to kill and be killed for the benefit of a few in the ranks of aristocracy they must be given a purpose. Nobody fights for another's profit but instead for his or her own, be it money, land, or spiritual reward.

So, one can see where leadership, the elite, use the lure of riches and spiritual reward to manipulate the rest of the population into following them into disastrous conflict with other nations and peoples. For many Christian scholars and priests warfare is not the will or liking of God, but the will and desire of men to control and dominate all others. In fact, some, like this author, suggest waging war in the name of religion is to use God's name vainly—to violate his holy commandment in that regard.

For many historians, anthropologists, and sociologists the wars waged by kingdoms under the guise of God's will are pointed out as examples of religion as a dark tool to control the masses, maintain power, and conduct wars for gain against other peoples. Some, but certainly not all, assert in their public lectures, books, documentaries, and classrooms that religion does nothing good for humanity and it is obsolete with the rise of the scientific method. Such could not be further from the truth, though.

These people seem to look too simply and draw their conclusions without accurate and detailed examination of the true causes of religious and other warfare. All wars and acts of organized violence have a particular goal related to the acquisition of resources, security, or dominance. Humanity exists in a dual dance between good and evil, potential and deed. When people decide to do good to others they justify it with their religion and they do the same thing when they endeavor to unleash their evil side.

What do Protestants believe that make them different, or unique, in comparison to the other Christian faiths? The founders of Protestantism had specific objections to certain institutions and practices of the western Catholic Church. Among them was selling indulgences for the sole purpose of financing extravagant building projects and lifestyles for the papacy and numerous bishopric offices of Europe. Another was the dispute between the concepts of *sola gratia* and *fides caritate formata*.

The four main Protestant movements were the Lutherans, Calvinists, Anglicans, and Anabaptists. Each group, though slightly different, held certain core beliefs and principles that united them under the banner of

What is Religion?

Protestantism. Some views and interpretations were completely opposite of those taught and held sacred by the church of Rome. The rejection of transubstantiation by Protestants is one adopted concept that was completely opposite of and in absolute conflict with Roman Catholicism.

Transubstantiation is a Roman religious concept that states the bread and wine of the eucharistic meal literally transforms into the actual body and blood of Jesus Christ. Obviously, anyone who has participated in Roman mass knows the bread is still bread and the wine is still wine after the eucharistic blessing. For reformers the Vatican was completely incorrect and missed the point made by Christ during the Last Supper. The concept of "real presence" was born from this group.

Real presence is a concept whereby the communion blessing invokes the spiritual and actual presence of Jesus Christ in the environment in which it is celebrated. According to this belief the bread and wine are, as they were in the Last Supper, symbolic reminders of what Christ did to save humanity from eternal condemnation. The spirit of God is present as we remember, through communion, the sacrifice he made for humanity.

The United States constitution includes two things that are unique among governments around the world and throughout history. The first is a requirement that church and state be separated and uninfluenced by each other. The second was to preserve the right of the citizenry to believe as they wish and to religiously practice as they believed.

The founders of the United States decided, based on history in Europe, it was necessary to ensure the government could not act under religious decree or bias and that the many religions of the world could not manipulate and use government to harm other faiths. In addition, they saw a necessity to ensure citizens were permitted to assemble, pray, practice, and build temples in accordance with their belief, and not as a central national belief as existed in Catholic Europe.

This desire to ensure the right to religion and the separation of religion and governance came from an awareness of the Protestant Reformation. Many of the founding fathers were Protestant, but some were of other faiths, including Judaism. They were well aware of the Vatican's efforts to have Luther, Wycliffe, Calvin, and other reformers executed as heretics. Had it not been for the agreement of German and Swiss princes, the Vatican would have squashed the movement entirely.

Without the Protestant Revolution would the United States constitution look the same as it does today? Certainly, coverage of the freedom of religion and the separation of church and state would be lacking. Perhaps there would also be a difference in the existence or wording of the articles regarding the freedom of assembly and the press.

How does science fit into Protestantism? In the beginning Protestants would stand beside scientists and scholars, demanding academic freedom in universities and specialty schools that were mainly run by the church of Rome. Many leaders of the Protestant Revolution saw scientific discovery as the discovery of God's work in nature and the universe and therefore advocated scientific and academic freedom. However, as time went by certain moral issues arose as science advanced and philosophies blossomed.

Like all other areas of Christendom, there are varying degrees of spiritual conservatism and liberalism spanning across the multitude of Protestant denominations in existence today. Some continue to state that science and religion are complimentary and neither should stand in the way of the other. But, other movements have begun to criticize science and philosophy. They see them both as undermining faith and encouraging sinful conduct among and by the people. Quite simply, medical science and the other sciences are viewed differently from one denomination to another.

Many churches stand in the middle ground, though. For these Protestants, science and its discoveries are primarily divine blessings but can be used immorally or wrongfully against humankind or the environment. In regards to destructive or immoral use of science, the religious object. Their objections remain focused on the sinful use of science and its discoveries rather than on science and its pursuit of knowledge.

An example can be seen in how most Protestant churches see nuclear science. When x-rays are used to see inside the body to diagnose injury or disease then science is being used righteously and morally. When a nuclear bomb is detonated over a city then certainly there is a destructive, immoral, and grievously sinful use of scientific knowledge. One does not go to hell for being a scientist but for using science to harm others rather than helping humanity and serving the greater good.

Islam

Islam is the youngest of the three Abrahamic faiths and appears to be a hybrid of sixth-century Arabian polytheism, Judaism, and Christianity. The Qur'an, a holy book to Muslims like the Bible is to Christians, contains many identical stories from the Judaic Torah and Christian New Testament.

Many of its most holy shrines and structures were originally holy places for polytheistic belief systems. But it isn't a complete borrowing of other religious writings and beliefs. There are a number of unique beliefs and stories written in the Qur'an.

Its founder is known commonly today as simply Muhammad, but was born with the given name of Muhammad Ibn Abd Allah ibn Abd al-Muttalib. The name means Muhammad the son of Abd Allah who is son of Abd al-Muttalib. He was born in the city of Mecca on April 26, 570 C.E. His father, Abd Allah, died just before his birth while participating in trade-related travel. His mother, Amina, and grandfather, Abd al-Mutalib, raised him. Much of his early life was spent with a Bedouin wet nurse named Halima. It was believed the Bedouin tribes maintained the purest form of living and were sent there to learn the traditional ways before being returned to the city.

There is a religious story that states Muhammad was grabbed and cut open at the chest by two men. A black spot was removed from his heart and he was released. It is believed these two men were the archangels Michael and Gabriel, and the black spot on his heart is symbolic of man's tendency to commit sin. Thus, after the spot was removed Muhammad is said to have become sinless and above bias. This story is generally accepted as a miracle by Muslims around the world.

Muhammad was six years old (c. 576 C.E.) when his mother died and his grandfather died when he was just eight years of age (c. 578 C.E.). This left him in the care of his uncle, Abu Talib, who succeeded his grandfather as the head of the clan. Muhammad was truly an orphan at this point, but his uncle was at least supporting him.

While accompanying his uncle on a trade trip through Basra (in modern-day Iraq) he is said to have been approached by a Christian monk named Bahira. The story alleges that Bahira examined the young Mohammad for a mark of prophecy and found it between his shoulder blades. It is said Bahira recognized Mohammad as the prophet written of in sacred texts held in the monk's possession at the time.[5] For many Muslims, this is confirmation that Muhammad was the second coming spoken of in the books of the Christian New Testament.

---

5. It is important to note the Qur'an and other sacred Islamic texts fail to list exactly what sacred Christian texts were being referenced in regards to signs of prophecy, nor are any such signs mentioned in the New Testament or Apocrypha.

Science and Religion

The city of Mecca is located in modern-day Saudi Arabia and is the most holy city in Islam. Today, the city is large and receives much of its income from pilgrimages much like other tourist cities do. It is preached by Muslim clerics that Mecca has been an important trade route city since the time of Muhammad's birth. However, many archaeologists and historians state there is little evidence to suggest the city actually held such an important trade route and market position in sixth-century Arabia. But, it is here the revered and cherished Ka'aba is located.

Today, the Ka'aba is considered the most sacred item in Islamic belief and tradition. According to Islamic scholars and clerics, the Ka'aba was built by Ibrahim and his son Ishmael. It is cuboid in shape and constructed of granite stone quarried from the nearby mountains. The entrance has massive golden doors built by Ahmad bin Ibrahim Badr in 1979. This door replaced a silver door put in place by his father, Ibrahim Badr in 1942.

Although clerics and obsessive followers of Islam claim the Ka'aba was built by Ibrahim (Abraham to Christians and Jews) and his son Ishmael, the archaeological and historical evidence indicates this to be a fabrication of fact. The Ka'aba existed far before the days of Mohammad as a pagan shrine. Karen Armstrong reveals the structure was a shrine to a polytheistic Nabatean god known as Hubal.[6] It contained an additional 360 individual idols to lesser deities that represented each day of the calendar year. One of these lesser deities is named Allah.

Mohammad, the founder of Islam, was a part of the Quraysh tribe. This tribe was dominant in Mecca at the time. Specifically, within the Quraysh tribe, Mohammad belonged to the Hashim clan. It was this clan that was chiefly responsible for caring for the then paganized Ka'aba.[7] His father, who died shortly before his birth, was one of the people whose duties included taking care of the polytheistic rights, rituals, and maintenance of the shrine.

By virtue of his birth and being raised within the Hashim clan, Mohammad was exposed to religious ritual, thought, and meditation. Though it is claimed Mohammad was illiterate, this would be in sharp contrast to the majority of clerical or priestly families of the polytheistic and even Christian traditions of sixth-century Arabia. The Hashim clan, though minor in politics and finance, was distinguished by its religious role. They were chiefly responsible for looking after holy items like the then polytheistic

6. Karen Armstrong, *Islam: A Short History* (New York: Modern Library, 2000).
7. Malcolm Clark. *Islam for Dummies* (Hoboken, NJ: Wiley, 2003), 82.

Ka'aba and its many idols. Thus, it is highly unlikely Muhammad was illiterate or absent of religious/spiritual experience and conditioning.

Allah, the Muslim God, was originally one of many lesser deities within the Arabian polytheistic tradition.[8] He was called upon only in times of hardship. The chief god in this pantheon was Hubal, though. It is for Hubal that the Ka'aba was originally built. It is also a tradition of the time for each clan and to have a patron god looking over them. It is entirely plausible, though unproven, to say the lesser god, Allah, was the patron of the Hashimites and therefore quite familiar to Muhammad from his earliest days.

Although the history and archaeological trail clearly indicate Allah and the Ka'aba are products of pagan polytheism of early Arabia and are not the same god worshipped by the Jewish and Christian communities, Islamic tradition asserts that Muhammad was a descendant of Abraham and that he was chosen by the God of Abraham to be the final messenger. It further asserts the Ka'aba was constructed by Abraham and his son, Ishmael, even though there is no record of Abraham having ever entered the Arabian Peninsula.

Many of the beliefs held by modern-day Muslims are quite similar to those held by Christians and Jews. For instance, they are monotheistic and recognize only one, true god. They believe God created the universe and all that is in it. Muslims are forbidden to worship idols or other gods, money, power, or oneself. Like Christians, Muslims believe there will be an end times and that humankind will be judged in accordance with its deeds and misdeeds by God. Additionally, they believe salvation, or acceptance into heaven, comes through obedience and submission to God.

The term, "Islam," literally means to submit. Going along with that meaning and general label for the faith there are "those who submit to the will of Allah" and are known commonly as Muslims. So, to follow Islam is to submit to the will and revealed laws of Allah. What constitutes the will of Allah and his laws has often been a subject of heated, even violent, disputes between leading clerics and general followers for centuries. Entire governments have waged war over differences in Islamic interpretation and application.

All Muslims are required to not only declare, but to also believe wholeheartedly there is no god but Allah and Muhammad is his messenger. For the most part, this requires all Islamic believers to reject any and all other faiths, even if they are closely related and differ only in minor areas

8. Ibid.

of practice and doctrinal application. This is so within the ranks of Islam, too. There are many sects that disagree and violently attempt to eradicate opposing sects. The result has been the creation of cultures and kingdoms that are in constant inter- and intra-cultural conflict.

Constant in-fighting and uncooperative interaction within Islam have been the chief reason the many nations of the Islamic region (Middle East) have failed to unify their numbers and power. Each sect of Islam accuses the other of being *kafir*, meaning unbelievers of the worst sort. They do not see any difference between an atheist, who believes in no god whatsoever, and a follower of any religion other than their own. Many governments and non-Muslim cultures use this rigidity to maintain instability and control over the Middle East and parts of Asia.

In regards to worship philosophy and practice Islam has five pillars. They are commonly known as the Five Pillars of Worship. They are:

1. Testimony that there is only one God, Allah, and Muhammad is his messenger
2. Five daily prayers
3. Daytime fasting during the month of Ramadan
4. The giving of alms
5. One pilgrimage to Mecca in a believer's lifetime

Average Muslims suffice only to know the very basic concepts and teachings of Islam. They do not spend much time contemplating the greater or higher levels of the faith. Intellectual contemplation of beliefs and the reasoning behind them come secondary to absolute submission to the will and laws of Allah as described by an elite clerical hierarchy. Quite often the clerical elite are also among the political leadership of various nations. The theocratic state of Iran is a contemporary example of the dual roles played by Islamic clerics.

Because of the distractions of political and financial ambition many clerics and leaders have been placed in opposing positions from one another. The religious concepts of Islam are then applied in Machiavelli style in order secure power and control. Schisms within Islam have occurred primarily over differences regarding leadership and authority, rather than spiritual interpretation or beliefs. The emergence of Shia and Sunni Islam is a prime example of division based on power and authority rather than concepts of faith and practice.

What is Religion?

Muhammad died on June 8, 632 C.E. (Gregorian calendar) in Medina. His Lieutenants were just as ambitious, spiritually and politically, as he was and a struggle for dominance quickly developed between them. On one side were those who believed Muhammad should be succeeded by his cousin and son-in-law Ali, and on the other side were those who believed he should have been succeeded by the first three caliphs. From this dispute emerged two distinct sects of Islam.

Shia Islam believes Muhammad should have been succeeded by blood relatives and descendants. Sunni Islam believes the first three caliphs should be in charge. Of course, as each chose a side in the conflict, neither recognized the other as being Muslim. The choice was less based on belief and faith than on socio-political benefit or gain.

Shia Islam

Shia is the second largest faction of Islam today. Followers of this branch are often called Shi'is (Sheese), Shi'ite, or Shia. The term "Shia" is a shortened form of "Shi'atu Ali," which means the "faction of Ali." This group broke away from the larger Islamic community shortly after the death of Muhammad.

Ali, Muhammad's son-in-law and cousin, was believed to be the proper successor by this group of Muslims. It is from their support for Ali as successor that the name Shia is derived. Their objection to people outside of Muhammad's bloodline as leaders comes from a belief that only God can choose his messenger and the successor to his messenger.

Shia Islam can be found all over the world but is centered mainly in countries such as Iran, Iraq, and Afghanistan. This order of Islam has followed a lineage from Muhammad, through Ali, and on down to al-Mahdi. The al-Mahdi is considered the last imam who mysteriously disappeared and has never been discovered. Many believe he will return during the days of last judgment along with Jesus.

It is this belief in the return of al-Mahdi that drives the current policies and actions of Iran's theocratic leadership. Well-known and knowledgeable Iranian dissidents have claimed Iran's regime is seeking nuclear weapons in order to use them against those they see as enemies of Allah and to bring about the chaos of the end times. For President Ahmadinejad the goal is alleged to be the destruction of the world in order to bring about the return of al-Mahdi and the times of paradise. His rhetoric certainly does seem to show an inclination towards such a belief and goal.

One cannot judge the entire Shia populace on the radical beliefs of a few. It is important to state firmly that many within Shia Islam refuse to believe the al-Mahdi can be made to return through sinful and disastrous human actions. These people also oppose the current regime and reject their radical Islamic interpretations. It is a deadly game to oppose those in absolute power, but each year many put their lives on the line to correct an abuse of Allah's teachings and commandments.

What we see within Islam, as is seen all around, is a struggle by and between human beings for power and control. It is not the religion but how it is applied and preached by people. Shia Islam alone has several hundred sub-groups and many clash on interpretation, use of violence to perpetuate and spread the faith, and issues of tradition. There are factions who are humanitarian, peaceful, and able to cohabitate with others, and then there are those who are rigid, unaccepting of other beliefs, and use violence to achieve their goals.

If one argues religion is the root cause for humanity's evil deeds, then one would have to demonstrate some level of consistency. What I mean is if religion is nothing but the dark side of humanity, then it will consistently lead any and all followers or believers to do disastrous and evil things. But, this is not seen in this religion. What occurs in Islam is the same that occurs in Christianity and Judaism—there are good and bad individuals within their ranks of believers. That illustrates clearly that it is the choices made by individual people and not the doctrines of faith that allow for and enact good and ill will.

Sunni Islam

Sunni Islam comprises between 80 and 90 percent of the world's Islamic population. Of course, this is the general classification of Sunni Islam and encompasses all of its subdivisions. It is difficult to pinpoint which Sunni sub-faction is largest or most dominant.

Sunni Islam came into being at the same time as Shia Islam. In fact, it was the difference in opinion regarding the successor to Muhammad that brought both into existence. As is written in the preceding section on Shia Islam, there were differences between its scholars and leaders regarding who or if someone should succeed Muhammad. The Shia, of course,

What is Religion?

believed Ali should succeed him, but the Sunni believed the original three Caliphs should lead in Muhammad's stead.

Over time, these differences would give birth to differing traditions, opposing interpretations, and ultimately violent clashes. However, the basic traditions and original interpretations and teachings by Muhammad have remained the same throughout Islam. From this perspective, Sunni Islam and its relationship with Shia Islam can be viewed in much the same way as how Protestant Christianity interacts with Roman Catholic Christianity. There are minor differences in one area and major differences in others.

What has brought about this split in Islam? We are all told it was an irreconcilable difference within the leadership regarding who should lead after Muhammad's death. But, what ultimately leads to an impasse in theological negotiation? It isn't so much *what* than *who* is behind the impasse. A rigid person is unwilling to negotiate or compromise with others. When such rigidity takes form in any discussion we see impasse. Thus, the religion of Islam has basically remained the same but has two different leadership forms due to leaders who are unwilling to compromise. It isn't faith in Allah or the teachings of Muhammad, but the rigidity common throughout humanity that has led to division, ugly arguments, and violent clashes. Again, it is people and not religion that has led to the less admirable traits of spiritual behavior in humankind.

Sunni Islam is not without its own radicals and violent behaviors, though. Like all faiths and belief systems, there are those who hold to strict and rigid interpretations and methodologies. Many of such spiritual positions and practices are unhealthy and threaten the peace established within the broader concepts of faith. But, these are the doings and socio-political beliefs of humankind and not the established teachings of any particular faith. Where a person's religion teaches and commands peaceful tolerance of other beliefs the individual becomes rigid and forceful against all who do not believe as they do. More often, religion is stolen and mutated to fit the whims and wants of military and political leaders seeking power and control.

At present, Sunni's are among the leading directors and members of many of the world's greatest Muslim charities and missions. In spite of the fact that people like Osama bin-Laden and many other terrorists come from Sunni Islam, the majority are peaceful and compassionate followers. They reach out to others, Muslim and non-Muslim equally, in times of disaster or great need. Many of history's greatest poets, explorers, scientists, and philosophers are Sunni Muslim.

Again, we are all left looking at this religion just as all the others have been. In order to say it is innately evil there must be consistency between religious concept and inhumanity. But, there is no such correlation. What *is* seen is a spiritual concept followed by many individuals. Each has their own way of seeing and applying that concept, and, unfortunately, some tend misuse and abuse. It is not faith but the individual who makes the difference between good and evil.

Today, Sunni Islam continues to suffer violence at the hands of radical Shia Muslims. Of course, there are those within the Sunni denomination who have reciprocated it. The primary basis for this violence is the differences between the two main elements of Islam. Chiefly, radical Shia have accused Sunni Muslims of being non-believers because they do not accept the idea that Islam should have been led by the descendants of Muhammad. Of course, the exact opposite is asserted by the Sunni against the Shia.

Sufi Islam

Sufism is a mystical or spiritually meditative form of Islam. As is the case throughout the Muslim community, Sufis are accepted by some groups and rejected by others. The two main denominations of Islam, Sunni and Shia, do not claim Sufism as keeping with Islam. Sufis are generally more peaceful and prefer to view all things in nature and between men as gifts from God or manifestations of Allah.

Sufi followers and clerics describe this practice as a science by which one sheds himself of evil ways and sin and leaves room for nothing but Allah. Basically, the mystical and deeply spiritual views taken by its practitioners are what construct the defining factors of Sufism. One of many unique traditions seen in Sufism is *dhikr*.

Dhikr is the process of repeating all the holy names of Allah through meditative chant. This can be compared to the chants of Buddhist monks or the rosary prayers in Catholicism. The idea is to create a meditative zone by which one is cleansed of sin and focused on absolute surrender to Allah. Beads, resembling the Orthodox Christian Chotki, are often used during the dhikr process.

Because all things are viewed as either a gift from or a manifestation of Allah, science is embraced and studied. Medical science and engineering

What is Religion?

are utilized frequently and understood as a tool for humankind and not something that debunks or clouds one's ability to believe and commune with Allah.

What is of unique interest regarding Sufism is it is practiced and spans across both Sunni and Shia Islam. Although Sunni and Shia groups and scholars argue constantly and even engage in violent exchanges, they come together under the practice of Sufism. In this sense, Sufism isn't a separate or third party form of Islam, but rather a practice of meditative reflection and surrender to Allah that exists in both of Islam's main elements.

Another unique trait of Sufism is the tendency to become ascetic in practice and lifestyle. From a distance, this leads many to compare Sufi clerics and strict adherents to Christian or Buddhist monks. To a degree it is true that Sufism represents the closest thing to monks seen in Islam. But, asceticism isn't a requirement in Sufism, and thus it is a general practice that has numerous orders to it. Some are rather monk-like while others are more community oriented and open in practice.

Because of its mystical qualities one would think it impossible for followers to become radicalized and violent in the enforcement of their beliefs and practices. This is, in many cases, the truth. But, quite frequently the contemporary world is disrupted by violent attacks and bombings by Sufi-oriented Muslims from both denominations. Why?

It is always hoped that because both Sunni and Shia Muslims practice Sufism the two will be drawn out of their schismatic state. But, this has not occurred and instead the Shia-originated Sufis tend to believe concretely and radically in the Shia as the only way while Sunni-originated Sufis tend to become more rigid in their Sunni perspectives. The result has been the creation of radicalized members within each major sect rather than an increased inclination towards reconciliation. However, it is important to know the radicalized elements within Islam remain a very small group and do not represent the majority of Muslims nor the main applications and interpretations of Muhammad's teachings and revelations from Allah.

The majority membership of Muslim communities within the Shia and Sunni sects refuse to recognize Sufism as a truly Islamic belief system or practice. These same elements also tend to reject the use of violence to achieve Islamic conversion and conquest goals. So, Sufism, like radical Jihadism, has become a small and odd little group on the fringes of the Islamic faith.

Science and Religion

The ascetic practices of Sufism along with its mystical interpretations are often exploited by terrorism-oriented Islamic groups around the world. It is used to draw appeal in recruiting and in conditioning members mentally for the violence they commit. It is even used to justify the violence altogether. However, if practiced properly, Sufism generates inner peace and general appreciation for all that has been created by Allah.

If followed in accordance with its intent, followers learns to view all things and people as creations of Allah. The believer in this form of Islam accepts what happens as the will of Allah and does not seek to disturb or otherwise alter the natural condition of things. Their meditative practices, combined with their spiritual view of the world, allows them to manifest personalities that are open, non-destructive, and tolerant. It is a very small group of twisted people who take and abuse this otherwise charming and peaceful philosophy of spirit.

Ahmadiyya Islam

Ahmadism is a reformist variety of Islam that was founded in British-colonized India on March 23, 1889 by Mirza Ghulam Ahmad. The movement gets its name from the founder's last name. The denomination is known as Ahmadiyya and its followers are often referred to as Ahmadis or Ahmadi Muslims. Ahmad was succeeded by another leader following his death in 1908.

What makes this religion unique is it appears to be a nineteenth-century hybrid between mainstream Islam, Christian missionary doctrine, and another faith known as Arya Samaj. It recognizes the birth, death, and resurrection of Jesus and his prophesied return, like the Christian community does. But, Ahmadis believe Mirza G. Ahmad was the second coming of Christ. They equate, or appear to equate, the Al Mahdi messiah of Islam to the Christian Jesus Christ. This has led many within mainstream Islam to reject Ahmadism entirely. Christians have the same difficulty in accepting the claim that M. G. Ahmad was the second coming of Christ.

After the death of Ahmad, the Ahmadi community strongly disagreed about who should succeed him as leader of the faith. In a situation that almost exactly mirrors the schism between Sunni and Shia Islam many years before, the Ahmadi's also split over succession and leadership issues. One group, the Lahore Ahmadis, believed the movement should be led and guided by an Anjuman (a body of holy scholars) while the others believed

What is Religion?

the Caliphs appointed by Ahmad should lead the community. No agreement could ever be reached and thus the two bodies of Ahmadism, Lahore and Ahmadi, were born.

Ahmad taught that Islam, mainstream Islam, had lost focus on the true teachings of Muhammad and the essence of Islam. He, and his followers, believed Islam was too divided, and shouldn't resort to violence, but peace. They also saw the rigidity and intolerance of mainstream Islam as offensive to Allah and counter to his directions of peace and love, tolerance and acceptance, and complete surrender to Allah's will. It is because of this view that modern Ahmadi's see themselves as leaders in restoring the original and true essence and practice of Islam as revealed by the prophet Mohammad. They reject radicalization within Islam entirely.

As a result of their peaceful beliefs, belief in the return of Christ and al Mahdi in the form of M. G. Ahmad, and their tolerance of others, they have been utterly rejected and persecuted by mainstream Islam. Ahmadi's have been tortured, murdered, imprisoned, and bombed by Shi'ites, Sunnis, and Sufis alike. Many fatwas have been issued against Ahmadism, and mainstream followers are ordered by their religious leaders to kill any Ahmadi they find—on site.

Contrary to the desires of the violent objectors to Ahmadism, there has been no eradication or suppression in growth. The exact opposite has occurred in the face of oppression and execution, and Ahmadi Islam has grown into the millions while spanning across two hundred nations. Lahore Ahmadism is also rather large but spanning across only a few countries. Like Jesus and his followers, Ahmadis are only strengthened in their determination and perseverance under the torment and threat of persecution. Ahmadiyya Islam was the primary Islamic religious practice among African Americans through to the 1950s.

They have proven peace and love prevails over violence and hatred. Ahmadism is simply incompatible with terrorism and spiritual rigidity. It seems to maintain focus on the peaceful teachings and directives of Allah and his holy messenger Mohammad.

In regards to scientific activity and discovery, Ahmadism is of great compatibility. It views all things as either creations or revelations of Allah. Thus, science is seen as a holy attempt to gain oneness with Allah and discovery through the scientific method done in accordance with the will of Allah. As a result, science, especially medical science, has become rather common among Ahmadis in Pakistan and India. Science is absolutely embraced as a holy pursuit and by no means condemned by Ahmadis.

Karijite Islam

Karijite Islamic practice and belief poses the greatest threat to inter- and intra-cultural peace and stability. Its extreme Islamic views and absolute rejection of all outside faiths has led to extreme acts of violence and oppression. Karijite philosophy comprises a significant amount of the justification used by extremist radical Muslims who resort to violence and other immoral acts against others.

Although this form of Islam is often characterized as a separate denomination, it is nothing more than a theological interpretation applied within Islam. Like Sufism, Karijite practice does not stand alone among the other Islamic denominations, but rather it permeates throughout the two main denominations as an extreme philosophy and practice. Karijite theology is practiced by both Sunni and Shia members.

Karijite Muslims consider all other non-Karijite sects as blasphemous and non-Islamic. They reject fellow Muslims as much as they reject all other religions of the world. They believe anyone who does not practice Karijite Islam is deserving of death. The result has been a long and voluminous history of persecution, oppression, war, and terrorism.

For the rest of Islam, Karijitism is seen as absolute perversion of the will of Allah and the teachings of Mohammad. Indeed, it does appear its adherents are more interested in violence against others than in spiritual enlightenment and entry into the paradise of heaven. Karijite belief is a prime example of how humankind imperfects and perverts the perfect. They have taken something wonderful and, not unlike the great deceivers and demons described across the many religions of the world, have twisted it into a hateful, rigid, and wicked thing. This is an example of how twisted humanity can warp and misuse religion in a most deadly and disastrous manner.

Karijite beliefs are significantly different from regular or mainstream Islam. Their primary beliefs are:

1. They considered the Caliphate of Abu Bakr and Umar to be rightly guided, but saw Uthman ibn Affan as having deviated from the faith and subject to being killed.

What is Religion?

2. They believed Ali ibn Abd Talib commited a grave sin against Allah in the battle of Siffin when he agreed to negotiate rather than engage in combat. In their eyes a conflict could only be settled in battle and Allah decides the victor. Thus, they marked Ali for assassination because he did not do as they wished in seeking peace over war.

3. Karijites believe the act of sinning was the same as complete disbelief and rejection of Islam. Sinners in the faith were labeled kaffar (disbelievers), which carried a death sentence. The simplest infraction could get a person executed.

4. Karijites believe any pious person can be elected by the Muslim community as a caliph (leader) and reject the hereditary and original caliphate succession concepts of Shia and Sunni Islam.

5. They label all ordinary Muslims as non-believers (kaffar) because they accept the teachings and leadership of Caliphs, who were rejected and even killed by them centuries earlier. Remember, kaffar are subject to immediate execution and are not considered Muslim under Karijitist belief.

6. The Qur'an is seen as the primary source of Islamic and political jurisprudence. Certain Hadith are rejected because of the Caliph who wrote them.

Today, it is said by some that the Karijites no longer exist. But, according to Al-Shahrastani's fatwa, "Anyone who walks out against (seeking to overthrow) the true appointed Imam upon whose leadership the majority is in agreement is called a Kharjii."[9] In contemporary times there have been many people who attempted to overthrow appointed imams and establish extremist Islamic theocracies against the will of the governed.

Additionally, revolutions against established Islamic states and peoples have occurred, resulting in Karijite extremism, rigidity, oppression, and cruelty towards millions in places such as Afghanistan and Iran. There are no human rights, true democracy, or religious freedom in Karijite-influenced governments or societies. Even mainstream Islam sees this form of belief and interpretation as blasphemous and offensive to Allah.

Can anyone blame Islam for the existence of Karijiism? Is it the religious philosophy and tradition revealed by Mohammad or the directives of Allah that are to blame for this atrocious rigidity and embraced violence?

9. Al-Shahrastani, "Kawaarij," Fatwa Online, http://www.fatwa-online.com/deviantgroups/khawaarij/0010512.htm. (accessed 2012).

Or, is this the result of a twisted minority of leaders who have misled and misguided thousands of others? Indeed, it depends more on the person viewing and interpreting than the religion he or she follows.

Where do we see Karijites today? Unfortunately, the answer to that is *everywhere*. We see them flying planes into New York buildings, strapping bombs to themselves and detonating at bus stops in Israel, blowing up schools in the former Soviet Republics, and setting 155mm artillery shells as roadside bombs in Iraq and Afghanistan. They are wreaking chaos, destruction, oppression, and death everywhere under the false belief that what they do is endorsed by Allah and directed by the Qur'an. Men are responsible for this perversion of Islamic faith, not Islam itself.

Bahá'i Faith

Bahaism is considered Abrahamic because it accepts Abraham as a prophet of God. But, this isn't where the similarities with Christianity, Judaism, and Islam end. Baháism is a progressive, monotheistic religion that emphasizes the unity of humanity and religion.

It interprets religious history as a series of divine revelations through prophets of various religions. Each prophet, be it of Judaic, Christian, Islamic, or even Buddhist origin, is seen as a messenger or manifestation of God. Each religious tradition and prophet is considered necessary for the time in which they existed or were founded, but belief and adherence to the one true God evolves over time. Humanity's relationship with its creator also evolves and grows over time. So, certain elements of Judaism, Christianity, Islam, and Buddhism (to name just a few) have been accepted and incorporated into this religious belief system.

Baháism has its roots in Shia Islam and was founded in nineteenth-century Shiraz, Persia (modern-day Iran). The Bab (or "the gate") was the original teacher and recognized prophet of the religion. He was executed in Tabriz, Persia in 1850. Prior to his death the movement and its adherents were known as Babi's. However, this name changed after the death of the Bab's successor, Bahá'u'llah, to Bahá'i Faith.

Many academic professionals assert that Bahá'i Faith, because of its acceptance of all previous prophets from a number of different pre-existing religions, is nothing more than a theological cocktail. Such labeling is erroneous in view of the fact that this spiritual belief system has its own individual and independent prophets, teachers, and holy writings that exist in no other form of faith.

The Scriptures unique to this faith include the writings of the Bab, Bahá'u'llah, Abdu'l-Bahá, Shoghi Effendi, and the Universal House of Justice. Authenticated speeches and special discussions by the Bab, Bahá'u'llah, and Abdu'l-Baha are also documented and canonized. None of these addresses or sacred writings exists in any other religious institution of the present or past. They all originated within the Bahá'i Faith. Thus, this religion certainly stands alone and is unique, but is also related to other, mostly Abrahamic, faiths.

To many among the Bahá'i Faith, the Abrahamic religions of Judaism, Christianity, and Islam are not different in faith but in time. One seems to secede the other, starting with Judaism and ending with Islam. They believe their faith to be the latest manifestation of the same God worshiped by the others. Thus, Judaism, Christianity, Islam, and now Bahá'i include messengers relevant to the will of God for the time span in which they came. This is difficult to accept by the members of these three primary Abrahamic faiths who have argued and shed blood over the conflicts between their prophets and dogmatic doctrine.

What further distinguishes Bahá'i Faith from the other Abrahamic belief systems is that its followers believe the end-times prophesies of Judaism (judgment day), Christianity (Christ's second coming), and Islam (al mahdi) have all been fulfilled in the coming of their second leader, Bahá'u'llah. This is not unheard of as there are many contemporary and historically scattered assertions and beliefs. Thus, there is even greater rejection from Judaism, Christianity, and Islam.

Bahá'is, in their founding country Iran, are under constant persecution from radical Muslims and the government alike. Many are attacked and killed or imprisoned unjustly because of their belief. As a result Bahá'is worship and practice their faith clandestinely but have not been wiped out. Additionally, Bahá'i Faith temples can be found across the globe. They are currently present in two hundred countries, including the United Kingdom and United States where religious diversity is accepted and even protected.

Although the Bahá'i s have been subjected to great violence and oppression in countries such as Iran, Iraq, and Afghanistan, they have not retaliated with violence or discriminatory activity. This is because violence and intolerance are absolutely rejected by them. Bahá'is possess a strong desire for all religion to be acknowledged as worshiping same universal

Science and Religion

God through the teachings of various prophets. They seek peace and unity over division and conflict. It is a behavioral choice of both the individual and group adherence.

In regard to science, Bahá'i Faith is quite supportive. In fact, the discovery of the mechanics of the world and universe created by God is a requirement in the pursuit of divine revelation and closeness. There is no condemnation of scientific research and discovery alone. Where humanity misuses these discoveries to cause harm to others or life in general is where objection and condemnation are provoked. Service to God and humanity is a requirement of this faith and science, especially medical science, is a means to achieve this. From this perspective, science is not sin and is even noble, but the way in which it is used by humankind can be either good or bad—it depends on humanity as to whether science serves or destroys.

Indian-Rooted Religions

The term "Indian-rooted" when applied to religion is inclusive of a large number of independent and intertwined faiths that have begun in today's India, Pakistan, and Nepal (the Indian subcontinent). The list is tremendous and putting them all in this book would serve only to confuse and misdirect the reader from the topic of religion and its relationship to and consideration of science. Most of today's Indian religions sprang from one of four main faiths: Hinduism, Buddhism, Sikhism, and Jainism.

Hinduism, being the oldest of the four, is derived from the ancient Vedic belief system. These early Indo-Aryan people developed texts that were redacted and commented on by later religious scholars. Four Vedic Scriptures have survived and are known as the Vedas. The Vedic period stretches from c. 2000 B.C.E to 1500 B.C.E. Abraham is thought to have been born in 1800 B.C.E. This places Hinduism as being roughly three hundred years older than Judaism. They have both been around for a very long time, and Hindu traditions may have been among those preached against by the early Semitic monotheist prophets.

Buddhism originates from the Hindu schools of philosophy and dates back to c. 250 B.C.E. This was during the time of the Maurya Empire that united the Indian subcontinent. It was Ashoka who promoted the spread and acceptance of Buddhist philosophy and tradition throughout India after Maurya unification. Like Hinduism, Buddhism has managed to spread well beyond the boundaries of the Indian subcontinent and can be found

What is Religion?

throughout the world. Primarily rooted in Asia, Buddhists and Buddhist temples can also be seen in North America and Europe.

Other religions such as Sikhism and Jainism also root in India. Both of these faiths branch from Hinduism and are further based in the ancient Vedic philosophical principals. In order to ensure that the reader isn't "lost in the woods" only Buddhism and Hinduism will be covered in order to illustrate how religion in the Far East and science relate and coexist.

Hinduism

Hinduism is the oldest living religion in the world. Its history goes back to as far as the Neolithic (5500 B.C.E. through 2600 B.C.E) and is rooted in an earlier religious tradition known commonly as the Vedic Tradition. The Hindu traditions predate Christianity and Islam by millennia. Even Judaism is younger than this spiritual belief system.

Unlike many other world faiths, Hinduism is not a rigid set of philosophies and traditions but a conglomeration of different but similar concepts and practices. Also, there is no single founder for this polytheistic tradition as it has developed from numerous sources, the primary source being the Vedic Traditions. It is from the Hindu Brahman tradition that Buddhism is said to have derived.

Hindu beliefs are exceptionally diverse. This makes the formulation of a single definitive statement for the religious tradition impossible. This is because it doesn't have a single definition or spiritual view—there is no single, unifying creed or statement of faith. The very types of faith included in Hinduism are diverse; some sects are monotheistic, polytheistic, and even atheistic.

However, in this state of "everything and nothing" Hinduism grants absolute freedom of religion and belief. It does not shun nor persecute those who believe differently or worship differently. This is because Hinduism sees the world, humanity in its entirety, as one family. The one truth, which is spiritual sameness within humanity, is deified. Thus, they reject religious labels because they are seen as divisionary and counterproductive to humankind's spiritual development and unity.

There are a few general traditions and philosophies accepted throughout Hinduism, though. These are the concepts of dharma, karma, samsara, moksha, and the various yogas. Dharma is the concept of spiritual ethics and duty while karma is the belief in spiritual action and reaction (what goes around comes around). Samsara is the cycle of birth, death, and rebirth believers go through for many generations, millennia even, until they realize their soul, or atman, is the same as the supreme soul, or Brahman. Once this realization takes place then they are said to have achieved moksha (the liberation from samsara cycles).

In the contemporary western cultures of North America and Western Europe, there are many who believe in and claim to experience déjà vu. This is the feeling a person has seen or experienced a situation before. For many this means walking into an old plantation home (as an example) and recognizing it as a place they lived in or were very familiar with. It is as if it were a memory from a past life. This has left many within western Christianity and Judaism to believe people live in a cycle of birth, life, death, and rebirth similar to the Hindu and Buddhist concepts of samsara.

How do science and Hinduism relate? These two ideologies, one of spirit and the other of physical discovery and understanding get along very well. The ethics and standards of the scientific community can be seen in dharma; and the scientific concepts of social consequence, responsibility, and equal-but-opposite reactions can be found in the Hindu concept of karma. Enlightenment is sought by both Hinduism and science, through different approaches and views.

Buddhism

Buddhism has its origins in Hinduism, and even further into the Vedic Faith. More specifically, its roots are buried in the Brahmic elements of Hinduism. Its founder is an Indian prince by the name of Siddhartha Gautama, who abandoned the high life and comforts of royalty and accepted poverty and meditation. He taught primarily in the eastern part of the Indian subcontinent.

Siddhartha Gautama is believed to have been born at Lumbini (modern-day Nepal) in 563 B.C.E. An astrologer told Gautama's father, King Suddhodana, that the child would either grow up to be a great king or would abandon kingship and become a holy man if he sees what lay outside the palace walls. Suddhodana was determined that his son would grow to become king and forbade Gautama to leave the palace. However, containment wasn't successful. He was a naturally inquisitive person who sought to discover and uncover as much about the world and universe as he could. This isn't very different from many of history's most famous scientists and explorers. Siddhartha Gautama would manage to leave the palace on four occasions. Each one opened his eyes to the realities of the world and each one set him on a course of searching, learning, and enlightenment.

On Gautama's first outing he observed the suffering of the ordinary people. This was something he didn't see in the heaven-like environment of the palace. He was deeply saddened for these people and was deeply interested in ending suffering.

During his second and subsequent ventures outside the walls of the palace he encountered an old man and learned of aging and the suffering that comes with it. He learned of sickness and death, too. During his final exploration he encountered a holy man who seemed content in his life. This had a profound effect on Siddhartha, the prince, and he began to see the way to end suffering was to reject the material desires that lead to it. He also came to see that severing attachment to all things, even life, was an additional means by which one can be freed of suffering, sickness, and death.

Gautama abandoned the princely life and pursued a holy one. During his journey of enlightenment and liberation he studied at many spiritual schools and mastered many forms of meditation. But, he did not discover a means by which one could permanently separate from suffering. Thus, his search continued.

Eventually, Siddhartha decided to meditate until he reached enlightenment and separation from suffering. He did so beneath a special and indigenous fig tree known as the Bodhi Tree. He is believed to have been thirty-five years old when he vowed to meditate until enlightenment. According to some stories, Gautama reached enlightenment after many days of solemn and focused meditation. Finally, he had achieved enlightenment, detachment, and separation from suffering. Following this elevation into what is now known as the Buddha he continued to teach many followers. It was in Kushinagar at the age of eighty that the Buddha's physical body died.

Buddhism spread throughout India by 300 B.C.E. and reached its peak there during the Maurya Empire under Ashoka. Unfortunately, Buddhism began to decline in India following the rise of Puranic Hinduism during the Gupta dynasty but maintained a significant presence until the 1100s C.E. Today, Buddhism can be found throughout Southeast Asia and has been calculated to have as many as 350 to 500 million adherents worldwide.[10]

For many Buddhists, maybe even all of them, scientific discovery and research is not seen as bad. In fact, one might say discovering the workings

---

10. Perry Garfinkel, "Buddha Rising," *National Geographic*, December 2005, 88–109.

of the universe is a part of the path to ultimate enlightenment. The ethical and productive application of scientific knowledge goes hand-in-hand with service to humanity and separation from or the ending of human suffering on earth. Buddhism, like many of the other religions around the world, see wrong only when men misuse technology and science.

Many elements of the scientific community find themselves attracted to Buddhism because it promotes self-discipline, self-improvement, service to others, and the pursuit of enlightenment. Healing, comforting, improving, and educating humanity are the basic positive products of scientific research and applied science. Where they differ is where each dwells—one in the physical universe and the other in the spiritual universe. Since neither crosses into the other's path they co-exist to serve the human cause.

Clashes between the Buddhist and scientific communities occur only where there is immorality, enhanced suffering, or destruction of life and the harmony of life. Buddhists leaders would call the development of weapons sinful and heinous while the development of medicines and immunizations walk the right path. Some would see abortion as a sin, but medical procedures that protect the baby and mother during birth as righteous and good. Only those who are without morality, understanding, respect for life, and compassion for others would kill a child in the womb.

Buddhism does not condemn science or scientists because of their profession or existence, but it condemns the immorality among scientists and the wrongful use of science. A biologist who finds a cure to disease is wonderful, but another who develops bio-weapons is a demonic spirit of sorts. It isn't the method of discovery but the ill or well doings of individual people that makes good or bad for humanity, the world, and universe. Man's existence will not be extinguished by nature, but by man's misuse and abuse of nature.

Atheism, Agnosticism, and Irreligion.

In defining or discussing religion one must include AA&I, which stands for atheism, agnosticism, and irreligion. Over the many years these three terms have managed to develop and morph. In many cases they are ill defined and erroneously understood. For instance, many in the United States believe atheism is a lack of religious belief when, in fact, it is a belief absent of a supreme being. Some Buddhist and Hindu sects are *atheist religions*,

What is Religion?

whereby they have spiritual beliefs but do not believe in a supreme deity or pantheon of deities.

Agnosticism is simply saying one will believe in a god or gods when they see sufficient evidence it, or they, exist. Does this mean there are no spiritual beliefs in the heart and minds of agnostics? No, it doesn't mean that at all. Again, the Eastern religions of Buddhism and Hinduism promote healthy skepticism and close examination of assertions regarding a god or gods.

Where one finds a total lack of spiritual belief is in irreligion. The irreligious are those who have no spiritual beliefs whatsoever. There is no recognition of anything other than the physical. They possess no concept of the soul or spirits, of life beyond death, or any other spiritual state. In this there is definitely no belief in deities. When people, especially among North American Christians, use the word "atheism" they really mean "irreligion."

The Religions of Atheism and Agnosticism

Atheism

Atheism is a term that stands among the most misunderstood and misapplied in the English-speaking world. Today, many people think of atheists as people without religion or any spiritual belief system. Some people call themselves atheists, bashing spiritual concepts and beliefs. But, some atheists are misusing and misunderstanding this term. Atheism is not a lack of religious belief but of a belief in a supreme deity or deities. What? Can there be a religion that excludes belief and worship in gods? Can a person be religious and atheist?

Absolutely! There are many atheist religions, in that they reject the existence of a deity or group of deities but hold the existence of the soul and spirits to be true. Atheism simply means a denial of the existence of a god(s) and does not deny belief in other spiritual concepts or practices. In fact, atheism isn't a religion or even a replacement to religion, but rather a concept within religion.

How did the term and its definition, its true definition, develop? Its roots are in the ancient Greek word *atheos*, which means "without gods." It was used by the ancient Greeks to describe all people who did not believe in *their* gods, but it was never used to describe people absent of spiritual belief entirely. In other words, atheos was applied narrowly and from one, polytheistic perspective. The Greeks of long ago believed only their gods existed and to believe in anything else made one absent of the gods, but not absent of a belief. This sounds very familiar doesn't it?

Where else has the world seen theological rigidity? The belief systems that most frequently come to mind are the Abrahamic faiths of Judaism, Christianity, and Islam. In Judaism there is only one God who has created and controls the universe. The same belief held in Christianity and Islam is even stricter on the existence of only one true god. Anybody who believes or practices any other form of religious belief is seen as being without *their* god and therefore is *atheist*.

It was during the age of Enlightenment in Western Europe and North America that various intellectuals and theologians began to question the Judeo-Christian God. However, in questioning this deity they did not abandon or lack religious beliefs of another sort. Most Christians of the time were conditioned to believe there is only one true and absolute God and to believe anything else was to be godless. Thus, conservative Christians and their leadership labeled all beliefs outside of their own as atheism and their adherents as atheists. In those days one need only ask a question or challenge the church to be labeled an atheist and shunned.

This religious rigidity exists in all of the Abrahamic faiths and many other religions as well. Christians reject other faiths, Muslims demand adherence solely to their beliefs, and Jews think the same thing but from their theological perspective. Certain polytheistic faiths around the world are equally rigid in religious tolerance and dogma. Borneo is a prime example of "question our gods and get your head shrunk" rigidity. They all accuse each other of being atheists. So, atheism truly means, "you don't believe what I believe and because of that you are without god." But, it does not mean one is without religion or spiritual beliefs. It is a term of religious perspective rather than general definition or social classification.

To say there is no god and spiritual belief is folly is not to declare oneself atheist but rather irreligious. Irreligion, discussed later, is the absolute and complete absence of religious or spiritual belief. The irreligious reject all spiritual belief whatsoever and may even ridicule those who do have religious beliefs.

How do atheism and science interact? The answer to that is simply, the two are quite skeptical and inquisitive. When a scientific theory questions or even denies the existence of a supreme being it is in keeping with the atheistic religious perspective. Many atheists see humankind as being responsible for itself and the consequences of its actions. They believe, as many other religions do, that humankind is destined to advance and obligated to care for nature. These are also the chief principles of the scientific community. Atheism is easier for scientists as there is no god(s) to be offended by the intrusive nature of research and experimentation. When there are no consequences other than gained knowledge, even at the expense of life and environment, there is wide-open space for scientists of varying ethical principles to work their will without hindrance or responsibility.

Agnosticism

There are differences between agnosticism and atheism in that an agnostic does not reject the existence of a supreme being(s) completely. Instead, agnostics reserve room for the possibility for such an existence but lack sufficient evidence or knowledge that allows for full acceptance or belief in the existence of a divine entity. Many people fail to realize it is not just the lack of evidence supporting the existence of a god(s), but also the lack of evidence that solidly disproves a divine existence. In essence, these are the "I'm not sure one way or the other" people.

The term, "agnostic," was not coined by a theologian or other spiritual expert to describe the unconvinced yet open-minded people of the world. Instead, the descriptive was coined by a biologist in 1869. Like theism and atheism, agnosticism is derived from Greek. Although most English speakers pronounce this word as *ag-nah-stick* it is pronounced in the Greek tongue as *ae-nosis*. The prefix *a-* in Greek means "without" while the *gnosis* base word means "knowledge." So, to be agnostic is to be, "without knowledge."

Agnostics can be classified as static or searching. A static agnostic is one who isn't quite convinced one way or the other and is simply happy or content with that. Searching agnostics are continually seeking new information and experience that will eventually lead them to know whether or not there is or isn't a god(s). The seekers are known by this author as anazitisi agnostics. This is another use of Greek to describe someone on a quest for spiritual knowledge but has not yet acquired enough to commit to belief or rejection.

What many people tend to ask is whether or not agnosticism is a religion? The agnostic does not believe fully in a deity but doesn't reject it, either. Additionally, there are no traditions or customs of reverence or rejection among the agnostics. So, is it a belief, or a condition of confusion or uncertainty? It is a belief.

Among agnostics there is a belief that the existence of a god(s) is possible but unproven. This is accompanied by the counter-belief that such may not exist at all but, again, there is insufficient evidence to prove that. They believe knowledge is needed to understand this spiritual question and there is insufficient information (at present) to determine way or the other. In describing agnosticism the reader will see a heavy use of the words "believe" and "belief." This illustrates the fact that agnosticism is a belief—a belief in the possible but not absolute existence of a god or even spiritual realm.

The term "agnostic" was coined by the English biologist, Thomas H. Huxley, during a speech rendered before the Metaphysical Society in 1869. The term itself is not of theological consideration and construction but of scientific origin and orientation. Thus, it is quite fitting to the scientific thought process and discovery method.

Since the term was first used by Huxley it has become a topic of discussion and academic written works among theologians, philosophers, and social scientists. Agnosticism has been penned with numerous definitions and clarifications that now allows for confusion when applied by anyone. Today, agnosticism can mean a state of indecision, confusion, uncertainty, or indecisiveness. But its original definition, as rendered by Huxley in the nineteenth century, is it is a position whereby the person sees insufficient evidence to support or reject the claim of the existence of a deity (or deities) or any other claim of a supernatural form. In essence, like the movie *Short Circuit*, the person "needs more input."

If the Huxley definition is applied to agnosticism then we find an application of the scientific method to spiritual belief or disbelief. In essence, there are two opposing hypotheses. The first hypothesis is there is a supreme deity or a group of deities and that this element wields special powers and abilities that lay outside the normal laws of nature. The other opposing hypothesis is there is no deity or supernatural existence.

For the agnostic there is observation and testing of these hypotheses. In every attempt of consideration, contemplation, study, and experimentation the results have all been inconclusive. For the theist hypothesis, there is insufficient data to prove God's existence and the same conclusion stands for the atheist hypothesis. Thus, the individual is unable to conclude one way or the other and either leaves the conclusion as it is or continues searching for additional, more conclusive information on the topic. This is essentially the agnostic of original definition.

Obviously, when looking at science and its relation to agnosticism, it becomes quite obvious the two are nearly the same. The difference is in the application of science upon a particular subject in agnosticism as opposed to the general methodology and acquisition of knowledge through general science. But, they are exceptionally compatible. The essential element here is that agnosticism, like science, requires empirical evidence to support any assertion of divine or supernatural claims or of the rejection of any such claim.

Religion vs. Irreligion

Irreligion is often confused with atheism in modern-day usage. But, there is a significant difference between them. Irreligion is indeed a spiritual belief of a conclusive sort that stands alone and apart from all other belief systems, whereas atheism is more a status of faith or non-faith. Irreligion is the absence, complete absence, of religious practice and belief. There is absolutely no belief in any spiritual concept, dimension, or entity for the irreligious. For irreligion there is no need for proof of anything deitical or spiritual, as there are no beliefs or spiritual perceptions to compare or experience. An irreligious person simply exists and thinks in the physical world only because to them there is nothing more than that.

Atheism is often confused with irreligion because of its multi-category existence within the theological and philosophical spectrums. An irreligious person is, by the nature of having no spiritual conceptualization, an atheist. After all, an atheist says there is no God. However, as has been discussed earlier, atheism exists also within the category of religion and below that can be seen in any number of religions and religious movements. It is incorrect to say all atheists are irreligious but quite accurate to say all of the irreligious are atheist.

Religion, the presence of a belief in a supreme being and/or spiritual universe, has been discussed in some detail already. So, there is no need to define it here but rather to refer the reader back to that section of this book. Religion and irreligion are simply the descriptive terms for belief system presence in a person or group of people that stand at exact opposites to one another. Religion *is* while irreligion *isn't*.

Science and Religion

Can a person be atheist and religious? It is absolutely possible and absolutely present in many faiths around the world. In fact, Buddhism has sects that are atheist—meaning there is no God or gods, but a spiritual energy and presence through which one may join and advance him or herself. There are many other spiritual belief systems that exist without the inclusion of any superior or supreme being(s).

Is irreligion good for science and other academic pursuits? Although one would initially believe irreligion to be an open door for such activities, it really isn't. In a study of societies, past and present, we see irreligion is rare. Cultures that have graduated from primitive to advanced have done so through their wonder and desire to connect with their spiritual environment. In contrast, irreligious groups are generally short-lived and fail to advance. Why is this?

Many, indeed most, people who possess a religious belief tend to have feelings of destiny, being part of a larger and mostly invisible universe, and a genuine desire to discover their world and universe as it has been created or made to be by one means or another. Asking who, what, when, where, why, and how, they seek to understand their place in the environment and how they interact with it. First to come are the simple spiritual assertions that are enhanced or even replaced by more detailed examination and discovery (science) as the society evolves or graduates to higher levels of existence, understanding, and technology.

Irreligion tends to be in the here and now. There is little desire to uncover the hidden things because there is no reason or motivation to. These societies are very rare in humanity's history and tend to advance little. When the environment changes or disasters hit they are ill prepared as they have no idea of the *why* and *how* or *who* and *what* behind the event impacting their society. These groups fail to discover or realize their actions impact their future and the environment around them. The result is their own destruction, because a society absent of understanding (be it expressed spiritually or otherwise) is a society that lacks flexibility, ingenuity, and survivability.

Thus, an irreligious person or group can have a bit of a dulled blade in regards to creativity and ingenuity. Their sense of wonder and exploration tends to leave them rigid and ill adapted in times of stress and significant disruption. Their advancement slows or even stops as the old and less effective is kept in place while newer and better means and methods are never discovered. Advancements tend to be adopted from other groups or discovered entirely by accident. This is not a good environment or mentality for science to flourish in.

IS SCIENCE A RELIGION?

Many have asserted over the years that science is, in and of itself, a belief system—a religion of sorts. However, just as many people have asserted that science is nothing more than a means of discovery and the application of the discovered in everyday life. So, is science a religion or not? The answer to this lies in the means of definitive application and individual perspective.

Whether or not science is a religion has much to do with how people see and apply it in their daily lives. Basically, is there faith in it as an all-answering process or is it simply a tool used to discover and confirm new knowledge regarding the physical world? Some people see science as the only means by which the universe and humanity's purpose can be examined and defined. To these people there is belief that science gives all answers and anything beyond what it can define is false.

In addition, the amount of faith put into theories versus confirmed scientific laws has a profound impact on whether science is a mechanism of belief for an individual or group. This, of course, is dependent upon what definition is given to the term "faith." For some, faith is a belief in a spiritual concept even when there is little empirical evidence to support the belief. To others, faith is applicable to belief in anything, whether solid evidence supports the belief or not. For the purposes of this book, faith is seen as a belief in any concept even when no evidence is present to support it.

Faith should not be confused with delusion or delusional constructs. The difference between these two states of mind and belief is how evidence impacts the belief. A person who believes something to be true even when overwhelming evidence proves otherwise is a person who meets the definitive criteria for delusion. But, a person who believes in something with no supportive evidence and absent of solid refuting evidence is a person with faith. For instance, one can have faith in another person's successful performance in a specified task even though no evidence suggests the performance will succeed and there is an absence of sufficient evidence to concretely say the performer will fail.

It is unfortunate to hear contemporary professors and scientists say theory and law, within science, are one and the same. This is simply untrue and this development seems to be a form of regression regarding scientific standards and accuracy. A scientific theory is a belief not supported by fact, or it is not tested and confirmed to be fact. A scientific law, however, starts off as a theory but through research, observation, and experimentation becomes proven as absolute fact or a constant reaction to a given action or condition. In this, we see a very distinct difference between a scientific theory and a scientific law.

Having distinguished or affirmed the original intent behind the use of these two terms in regards to science we can now understand where science becomes tool or religion. In some cases it is both. Again, it depends on individual and group perception.

When a theory is seen, believed, and treated as a fact or constant in nature where no evidence through observation or experimentation supports it, then there is faith. When faith is present there is the opportunity and tendency to let it replace any spiritual or other, seemingly lesser, belief system in a person's life. Faith is the foundation of all religious belief constructs and in this application science certainly does become a religion for many.

In contrast, where a theory is seen as just a theory, there is no faith in it. For this person the theory is just a concept worth consideration and further investigation. There is no need for faith where something is known and demonstrated as fact. This is a case of science being what it has always meant to be—a tool by which the natural world is explored, discovered, and understood. In this regard, science is methodology and nothing more or less. It does not directly support or deny any other belief mechanism or construct. After all, a camera doesn't prove or disprove God; it just records what is in the visible spectrum.

So, can science be religion? The short answer is yes, to some who place faith in theories science itself cannot prove or support. This condition is no different than the faith put into other theories of spirituality and universal understanding.

2

What is Science?

SCIENCE DEFINED

An Italian immigrant attempting to learn English in New York once told his instructor the English language was very difficult to learn and fully understand. When asked about his statement he replied saying English has a tendency to put many definitions and meanings to a single word. This is a very true situation in English communication, regardless of the nation or culture using it.

For instance, in the United Kingdom the term, "lift," can have many meanings. It can mean to elevate something from one altitudinal point to another or it can mean giving someone a ride in a vehicle from one point to another. Elsewhere, the same term can refer to an elevator, escalator, or even a bus. The applicable meaning to the word depends on how, when, and where it is used in spoken and written English.

The same is so for the word "science." This term also has many meanings and applications in English. However, it has the added twist of being an international term.[1] The problem with a single word, like "science" or "religion," having many meanings is there is much room and tendency for misuse and misunderstanding.

The modern word "science" is derived from the Latin word, *scientia*, which means simply, knowledge. In its earliest use, science simply referred to knowledge gained by humanity that was credible and provable. It had

---

1. An international term is a word that spans across many languages and cultures. A person from Spain can fly to Japan and use the word "science" and it will be understood with the same meaning by the Japanese.

nothing to do with the methodology applied to it today. In these early times, science dwelled well within the realm of philosophy. In fact, the philosopher Aristotle once stated, "science refers to the body of reliable knowledge itself, of the type that can be logically and rationally explained."[2]

Since the days of the great philosophers science has been closely related to philosophy. Sometime around the seventeenth century, in Europe, a separate branch of philosophy emerged and was labeled natural philosophy. From this came the modern academic subject of natural science. Natural science is, therefore, a body of reliable information that can logically and rationally explain natural things surrounding humanity, from the minutest element to the great expanse of the universe.

Through the likes of Johannes Kepler, Galileo Galilei, and Sir Isaac Newton the term began to take on a more specific application relating to the laws of nature. Newton's law of motion and other such discoveries are examples of this development. The universal theory of gravity is another example.

By the nineteenth century, in North America and Europe, science became more narrowly defined. Then, today, the term "science" is immediately recognized to mean the method utilized to acquire reliable knowledge. This methodology is also referred to as the scientific method.[3]

The broader definition continues to be used in modern times, though. The academic areas labeled library science, military science, and political science serve as examples of modern use of the older meaning of science. These are not disciplines whose knowledge comes from the scientific method, but rather from the more traditional philosophical perspective and means of examination.

Science, as a word, is often misused or incorrectly applied. The misuse is often generated by those who work in the realm of science, too. For instance, the academic area of theoretical science includes the incorrect application of the word science. Science is a body of knowledge that is able to be logically and rationally explained or concluded. Scientific data is not theoretical but rather established fact. In its other proper use, science is the means of discovering data that is reliable and provable. Again, there are no "I think this is it" concepts that can be accepted as science. A concept either is or it isn't reliable and logically or rationally explainable.

2. Aristotle, *Nicomachean Ethics.* Book IV (Oxford: A.T. Shrimpton & Son, 1981).

3. The scientific method is the disciplined process by which one acquires reliable knowledge.

Theoretical science is a compound of two opposing meanings: theory and fact. Something cannot be both unless, perhaps, the concept is partially based in established fact with a venture into conjecture. Thus, theoretical science is knowledge of theories upon which further examination and experimentation is warranted. But, it is not true science as it was originally and is contemporarily defined.

Theoretical science would be better stated as *hypothetical science*. This, of course, is more accurate but unnecessary as this has already been established within the scientific method as the hypothesis. This is an educated guess upon which experimentation and confirmation are performed by scientists or the baker around the street. One should always be aware of how science is being used, or misused, before placing a great deal of belief or faith in what is presented.

For the purposes of this discussion, science is defined primarily as the disciplines of natural science (geology, chemistry, astronomy, and biology) and the method employed to confirm knowledge. It is very easy for people to leave the realm of true science and enter the realm of hypothetical confusion.

Many people tend to place absolute belief in these unproven theories and hypotheses that render a position of more faith than science. It is through this confusion that a blurring of science and religion has occurred. This philosophical fog is where many incorrectly believe science is superior to faith or faith is superior to science.

A BRIEF DEVELOPMENTAL HISTORY OF SCIENCE

The Days of Men in Caves

To many it sounds funny to bring up the Paleolithic man and the scientific method in the same sentence. But, as hard as it is to believe, methodical science goes all the way back to humanity's earliest beginnings. It is an absolute fact that humanity has been steadily advancing from one generation to another, evolving, through observation, contemplation, experimentation, and confirmation.

Does this process sound familiar to the modern reader? It certainly should as contemporary humans recognize this basic pattern of discovery as the scientific method. What is known as the scientific method today was formally defined as late as the eighteenth century and refined by the later part of the nineteenth century. However, this was just formalization of what every human being in all generations has used since the species began.

In days long past humans observed things around them and thought, "If I do this then it will do that." With this thought in mind he or she experiments to test the idea and if it works it becomes new knowledge for him or her, the tribe, and many generations to come. If the experiment fails to confirm the idea then the early human goes back to the drawing board. This approach to learning and discovering has been very successful for humanity throughout history.

Developing the knowledge of earlier generations is nothing new, either. For instance, one generation may develop the stone knife, another the spearhead, and still a third will develop the arrowhead. With the development of the basic arrow came improvements such as the use of feathers to stabilize the projectile. Upon that came special shapes in the feathers to allow for a spin that furthers stability and accuracy. The same type of evolution took place with clothing, housing, medicine, general technology, spirituality, and even governance.

Science has been a part of human understanding and development throughout its entire existence. The method was there, but the modern label for it wasn't. It coexisted with spiritualism and spiritual philosophy throughout human history. What is interesting to point out is that in the earliest days of humanity there were no arguments regarding the spiritual beliefs of a community and the knowledge it discovered. These early people simply accepted the new knowledge as a revelation gifted by the divine and went on.

Pre-Philosophical Science

The term science is derived from the Latin term, *scientia*, referring to that body of knowledge that is reliable and logically and rationally explainable. There was no specialization or scope restrictions placed upon science in those early days. In those times, ancient even to that era, science was merely a body of knowledge that was reliable and could be used to discover new information and technology. It was not the creator of things, but the details of the things that had been created.

Additionally, there was absolutely no distinction between natural and spiritual knowledge. It was simply an understanding of the physical world as it was meant to be by those things that lay beyond current understanding. Both were considered reliable and articulated knowledge suitable to present and future generations. It will be quite some time before the standards of determining what is reliable information and how it is verified are developed.

The Greek term for knowledge, equivalent to Latin's scientia, is *episteme*. To those who have read or studied the Christian Bible, episteme stands out almost immediately. This is because the early church leaders, writing in Greek, would often write epistles. For instance, the epistle of Paul literally translates to "the knowledge of Paul the apostle." In these days, scientia or episteme was simply knowledge that was generally accepted as true and shared throughout the known world. Both spiritual and natural knowledge existed as science.

Philosophical Study of Nature

In the beginnings of the European philosophical era of science history the distinction between observed and demonstrable facts of nature and those of mythology remained intertwined. This is especially so for the pre-Socratic days. However, what marks the transition into the philosophical era of science history is the philosophers' focus on the "nature of things."

These early scientists often described how things were and what they did in their natural setting. For instance, the life cycle of plants and animals, balance of life, and properties of rocks and other materials were described and studied in detail. But, these same philosophers described the nature of love, hate, compassion, war, mind, and soul. There was no distinction or separation between the many subjects of the physical and the metaphysical.

The great philosopher Socrates applied philosophy and general explorative curiosity toward human things. He was interested in all things relative to human nature. Its behavior, interactions, development, and life were all subjects studied and written about by Socrates. He was also critical of the narrow view taken by physics regarding the presence of an intelligent order to things versus solely random circumstance of motion and matter.

Tradition and mythology were the realms of human matters and things during the days of Socrates. His reported observations and revelations regarding human behavior and interaction drew heavy opposition from his more traditionally and mystically rigid contemporaries. Eventually,

Socrates was executed for his philosophical revelations. This was primarily due to his separating or distinguishing human nature from divinity.

Another great philosopher of the classical times would emerge to restructure Socratic philosophy in order that humanity may be studied without causing a split from applicable spiritual philosophies. Aristotle would incorporate the nature of man with the divinity of man in his studies and contemplations. But, this did not hinder the discovery of physical things or things of nature.

Natural Philosophy in the Middle Ages

Aristotelian philosophy (or science) was the accepted approach to inquiries regarding natural and/or physical phenomena for many years. This teleological approach allowed for the divine and all of its related traditions to be considered and incorporated in the explanation and understanding of those things which occurred in the physical world and universe. This approach did draw a distinction between practical and theoretical philosophy, though.

It also allowed for certain observed facts to be dismissed and overlooked by authorities when what was observed in nature conflicted with what was spiritually believed through tradition. More accurately, it allowed for the rejection of people and ideas that were contrary to the desires and needs of the socially and politically powerful.

It has been postulated by many scholars throughout the last couple of centuries that man's rigidity began to raise its head and bare its fangs as early as the Middle Ages. However, heated arguments between the natural and spiritual philosophers/scientists existed prior to this period and there are moments of violence there, too. Where discovery, or enlightenment, conflicted with tradition, especially those traditions that kept the powerful in place, there was friction between men. Some accepted the discoveries and changed with them while others were less understanding and flexible causing them to reject it entirely. Again, this was almost always centered on maintaining political and social power rather than applied religious doctrines and beliefs.

We must also consider the fact that knowledge is power. Those in political and social power were easily threatened by those whose inquisitiveness allowed them knowledge of things that improved life conditions or enhanced technology. It is natural for humans to gravitate towards those

What is Science?

who provide answers, solutions, useful guidance, and effective leadership. In other words, innovators tend to rock the political boat after making big waves in the pond of culture.

It is primarily the political reasons and motivations that led to the persecution of history's great discoverers and philosophers. The Middle Ages was the birth of the most horrific persecutions of the sciences by politicians and princes seeking to retain control of their realms. Religion was the easiest excuse used to hide political maneuvering against a foe during these days, and historians have frequently made mistakes in identifying the true villain.

Though many historians and educators have accused religion as the root cause of the persecuted deaths of our greatest philosophers and discoverers, the true fiend is the human and not the human's religion. It is an unfortunate fact of human nature for a threatened person to act or maneuver so as to eliminate the threat, regardless of whether it is perceived or real. In many cases this will involve the misuse, misrepresentation, and abuse of cultural norms, laws, and beliefs. Certainly, it includes the bending and fabricating of facts to suit the individual or group's desired outcome.

It is no secret the Middle Ages were filled with strife and conflict by and between the many kingdoms of the time. There was constant political and military maneuvering and massive death was a common occurrence. Religion was used by political and military leaders to motivate troops and rally public support against external and internal enemies. It was also used to seize and maintain political power and/or influence. In general, religion was nothing more than one of many tools used to manipulate the masses available to and used by political leaders of the time.

However, this manipulative use of faith, or abuse of faith, was at the highest levels of the socio-political pyramid. On ground level, where the common people and simple priests existed, there was great belief in God and a genuine veneration for all of his nature. The same can be said for other faiths as well. At the common level, religion was no tool to accomplish worldly things, but rather a means by which one could acquire hope, maintain brotherhood, establish productive and moral living, and serve, while being served, by sincerely caring and loving people.

Many of the scientists/philosophers of the day were from among this group of truly moral and devoted religious people. They were not from the elite levels of leadership that controlled many cultures and kingdoms throughout Europe and the rest of the world. Few were even interested in the deadly dramatics of political intrigue. None of these people rejected or spoke against the existence of God but rather explained the mechanics of his physical world and universe.

When examining the writings of these great and gifted people we find true devotion and veneration of the divine with an understanding that the observed mechanics of nature demonstrated the immense complexity and glory of that which put it all in place and motion. Such views of scientific inquiry and discovery were not at all in conflict with the teachings of the predominant religions of the time. With this being the case, one is left asking why were they persecuted by high level religious and political authorities?

The answer to this question lies in the realm of human pride, greed, and politics rather than in religion or science. In the Middle Ages, as is the case even today, leaders maintained their power and control through a variety of means. One of those is through the tight control of information and in the use of misinformation. A misled and ignorant public is a controlled public.

When a person discovers or observes something in nature that allows for use of that information in a way that enhances life or provides advantage he or she draws attention to themselves from the general and leadership elements of humanity. This can be both positive and negative depending on the applied discovery's impact on society and cultural order. Sometimes, what is discovered and revealed to the masses is something the powerful wants to remain unknown to the general public they control. Many leaders, in fact all leaders, will use a people's ignorance against them in maintaining control and power for themselves.

In the Middle Ages, religion and devotion to the divine was seen by those in power as something that certainly needed to remain within their tight grasp. Thus, many of the church's leaders were the youngest sons of the most powerful families. Bishops, archbishops, cardinals, and popes alike were all cousins to a multitude of royal families and high-ranking ministers throughout Europe. This was certainly not by accident, nor was it of divine influence. This was the doing of men who were in power and sought to remain in power by all means. It was not of God, gods, religious philosophy, nature, or science.

With the established religions well under the control of the elite, science was left to continue the enlightenment of humanity. The institution of science academies under the patronage of princes and kings were quickly structured so as to allow only members of the powerful elite to be recognized. Like the institutions of religion, the powerful were seeking to control the scientific community and all knowledge it discovered. Such would continue through to contemporary times with significant success.

Discoverers not of the elite or dissident members of the elite were subjected to great persecution by authorities of science, religion, and politics when they publicized discoveries undermining established concepts. To demonstrate the earth orbits the sun, and not the other way around, created waves of doubt in the leadership and threatened to undermine their control and influence over the masses; this resulted in immediate attack, condemnation, and even execution. It wasn't the true teachings of religion or the discoveries of science that led to these executions, but rather the political, financial, and social leaders of the time who enforced these suppressions, omissions, and general public ignorance to maintain absolute control.

Regardless of persecution by leaders threatened by the knowledge science produced, there remained a series of people committed to the exploration of nature and the sharing of knowledge gained through these explorations. They did so at great personal risk not because what they did was offensive spiritually, but was threatening to established political and social leaders. Because of this, much of the discoveries made before and during the medieval period were destroyed or lost as inquisitors sought to enlighten humanity and politicians sought to manipulate and control humanity through its ignorance.

Much of the information acquired during this period was lost following the fall of the Roman Empire. There were a few, such as Isidore of Seville, who managed to preserve some knowledge through encyclopedic documentation. In other areas it was Syrian Christians in Eastern Europe who preserved scientific knowledge that would have otherwise been destroyed by controlling political and military leaders.

For instance, the Nestorians and Monophysites translated, preserved, and handed down the majority of knowledge acquired by the great Greek philosophers. Throughout Europe and Northern Africa, Christian monks, Jewish rabbis, and Muslim imams and scholars were responsible for the gathering and sharing general and natural philosophy and discovery.

Royal libraries of the time contained only those things that were approved by the elite controlling class and were never all-inclusive collections. Church and temple (Judaic) libraries and universities, though well under the control of the elitists, maintained complete collections and allowed for

Science and Religion

broader teachings because of the non-elite scholars and administrators who actually ran the institutions. This illustrates how it was not religion that persecuted science, but people who sought to gain and maintain absolute control and power over all others.

Renaissance Period

The meddling presence of human politics, greed, and pride within both science and religion continued throughout the time of the Renaissance. These hindrances to public understanding of nature's mechanics, and the divine will and intelligence behind their existence, continued to manifest as discoveries conflicted with manipulative disinformation issued by the leadership. Such information and enlightenment threatened to overthrow them through exposure of the masses to the truth regarding nature and God.

By the end of the Middle Ages and through to the early times of the Renaissance there was a large influx of eastern information in the form of scrolls and other documents. This was due to the collapse of the Byzantine Empire, from which many documents from libraries and government centers were sent west in order to protect them. Many scholars and religious philosophers also moved west in order to seek safety and a place to continue their work.

Those discoveries concerning the structure and mechanics of nature that were lost to Europe in the Middle Ages were relearned as eastern libraries and scholars became available. Not only were the ancient Greek teachings made available, but also newer information discovered by eastern natural and spiritual philosophers became available through documents and teachings by contemporary scholars and orators.

Technological advancements in Europe allowed for the development of the printing press. Books that once required monks to hand script were now stamped out in greater volume. Like today's internet, the printing press made information available to a multitude of people in a much faster time. More minds were enlightened to natural and spiritual philosophy, which led to more questions and the development of standardized approaches to discovery.

As a result of greater access to information many scholars began to move away from the Aristotelian philosophical concepts of nature and God. Bacon questioned Aristotle's ideas of formal cause and final cause and

What is Science?

emphasized the importance of experiment over contemplation. Descartes, like Galileo, argued that nature could be expressed mathematically.

The Age of Enlightenment

Knowledge and technology grew exponentially at the end of the Renaissance. The ideas of general education for all classes and the building of public access libraries began to take root. The old ways of Aristotelian philosophy gave way to a better and more fact-seeking methodology. Thus, in the seventeenth and eighteenth centuries human understanding of nature and spirituality changed drastically and traditional socio-political leadership had to show justification and supporting argument for their actions, or inactions, where they needn't say anything to those they led in the past. The ignorance of the merchant and even lower classes of society wasn't as abundant for exploitation as it once was.

A sense of freedom and a belief in the right of every human, regardless of wealth or class, to seek out and acquire reliable knowledge on all subjects began to manifest among the lay and scholarly alike. Critical thinking and comparative study became an increasingly present element of human thinking through all societal levels. This soon led to criticisms of established authority and resistance to archaic views, systems, and authority among and within the institutions of governance, academia, and religion.

With this realization of authority abuse and manipulation on the part of the leadership came resistance, and in some cases, outright rebellion by the oppressed. Such is inevitable when a society becomes better educated and aware of its surroundings. This, of course, resulted in suspicion and harsh reprisals by the elite against any subject who even remotely indicated disagreement or disobedience towards them.

Though historians like to blame religion for the persecutions suffered by the famous scientist Galileo, it is really the arrogance of the elite versus the enlightenment of the common that produced his political and social torment. Religion was only an excuse for the elite to make their attacks with the support of the masses. They wished to attack what threatened them while maintaining a clean public appearance. That political tradition stands in evidence even today.

What really happened between the papacy and Galileo, then? His persecutions did not begin as soon as he began to discover and teach those discoveries, but rather when he accidentally and quite innocently insulted the pride of a pope. In fact, Galileo was using a religiously correct position while the pope held fast to personal pride, a religiously incorrect position, when the problem all started.

Galileo had been commissioned by Pope Urban VIII to write about the Copernican system. The product of this project was a written work entitled, *Dialogue Concerning the Two Chief World Systems*. Galileo used arguments by the pope in this work and placed them in the words of a simpleton character. This, of course, offended the elitist pope and resulted in a tidal wave of angry reprisals hidden under the dress of faith.

Galileo's approach in this work was religiously and even dogmatically conformative and appropriate. It was the sinful pride of the pope and not God or Christ who started this unnecessary dislike and hateful treatment of Galileo. There was no disagreement in the work as the arguments came from the pope himself. Galileo was following the teachings of Christ in representing the holy teachings of a pope in the form of a simple, humble, and wise member of the common class. After all, Christ was common, humble, poor, wise, and perfect. This is what any truly Christian person, farmer or pope, strives to be; yet Urban VIII was far from it.

This scientifically gifted person wasn't the only victim to human jealousy and political intrigue. Almost all of history's persecuted discoverers show significant evidence of an offended or jealous leadership, more than any religious offense to whatever God or gods were worshipped at the time. It is pride, greed, arrogance, and ambition of man that persecuted others and not his religion or means of defining nature. It is here that historians tend to miss the reality of the situation and blame either science or religion for humanity's misdeeds against himself.

For politically skilled people, recognizing the importance of scientific justification for conditions and actions came to the forefront during the age of Enlightenment. Where religion was the authority upon which the politically and socially elite maintained power in the past, science began to take the stage. Where a political foe was once labeled a heretic he would now be labeled unscientific, unrealistic, irrational, or a religious zealot. The persecution remained along with the purpose of persecution—the elimination of socio-political competition by those currently in power.

What is Science?

IS RELIGION A SCIENCE?

Since science was given its formal and methodical definition in the eighteenth and nineteenth centuries, it has been seen as experiment-based and practical in comparison to religion where contemplation and speculation were applied. By the twentieth century faith was regarded as fact-less and science was seen as fact-based. This misconception made it easier for people to forget the two are brothers born from the same philosophical womb.

In contemporary times we have seen the blurring between science as pursuit of knowledge and science as explainer of all things physical and spiritual. This view makes science and religion competitors rather than distinct realms of human understanding. But, is this true? Is science also a religion?

To some, be they religious or non-religious, this is a ridiculous question while others, in ever-increasing numbers, place serious contemplation and practice into it. With the reversal of science confirmed by faith to faith confirmed by science came great confusion as to what subject belonged to which philosophical consideration. This seems to indicate what the individual believes of science determines whether or not it is his or her religion.

Science, or natural philosophy as it was once called, has traditionally sought to answer the questions of what, when, where, and how; religion has focused mainly on the questions who and why. Each examine the same phenomena in nature and attempt to define them mechanically and by means of purpose. In the strictest view of science, we quickly discover it is a means of discovery and experimentation that leads to reliable information on a variety of subjects and phenomena. It stays well out of the contemplation of who made it and why it exists, as this is the purview of religion.

With all of that having been said, people are beginning to worship scientific knowledge and those who discover it while completely disregarding the questions regarding intelligent design and control, or even purpose for existence. Many have forsaken the god of love and order for the god of chaos and statistical randomness. In this case, science, or at least scientific knowledge, has become a religion in and of itself where individuals and groups place faith in its ability to solve all problems and provide all answers. This is certainly a step beyond the boundaries of true science towards the bizarre application of physical rules on a spiritual universe.

Where followers of Buddhism, Christianity, Judaism, and Islam would reference and quote the Bodhisattvas, Jesus Christ, Moses, or Muhammad, the scientifically religious will counter with the theories of Copernicus,

Galileo, Einstein, or Darwin. Though many of history's great scientists would resent being worshipped and elevated to an apostolic level, generations of scientists and science-faithful have done just that.

How often are statues erected and intellectual temples made to those whose contemporary students venerate them as super-human, perfect beings? Universities originally founded and run by Christian monks and priests find their saints and apostles replaced by busts of Oppenheimer and Einstein. What has occurred is the institution of the spiritual veneration of human explorers as religious prophets, rather than as scientific explorers and definers of natural phenomena.

The true genius and achievements of Einstein were overshadowed by his mythos throughout this new science religion. In simpler terms, science treated as religion does happen, but it is a perversion of science and not the invention or clarification of religion.

What about faith? Is it also science that develops reliable information or is it a whim of imagination? The explanations of who and why things exist and interact tend to come from religious interpretation or other forms of philosophical contemplation, rather than coming from methodologies applied to physical understanding of nature. Faith, like the physical sciences, is based not on empty imagination, but on observation, experience, experimentation, and confirmation.

There are six points to a complete understanding of any subject, regardless of whether it is of physical or spiritual essence. These are the answered questions of who, what, when, where, why, and how. The questions why and how are often mixed-up by scientists and the science faithful. The words "who" and "what" are often incorrectly understood in forming a complete understanding of things, too.

If one were to ask a scientist why the earth was made he or she would most likely go into the physical details of planetary formation and the role of gravity. If this same scientist was asked why the universe exists he or she would most likely describe concepts of the Big Bang theory and the constant expansion of matter throughout the emptiness of space. But, these aren't answers to why, but rather to how these things came to be. The reason for this is that there simply is no "why" in science. They know and focus solely on how; and thus, for the irreligious scientist, confusion occurs between the questions why and how. This is true for virtually all why questions, too.

On the other hand, if one were to ask a Christian priest or minister the same question, why the earth was made, an entirely different answer is rendered. In this scenario the how is seen as a mechanism of divine will and this will of the divine is the why behind earth's existence. Of course, divine will has a multitude of views and definitions, but among all of these doctrines, definitions, traditions, and perspectives remains the identification of *purpose behind means.*

The same situation exists in the questions of who and what. Again, if a natural scientist were asked who created the universe an answer consisting of the theories and laws of physics and the interactions of objects would be given. Physical science focuses on the what rather than the who of existence and the functions of nature. However, if a cleric is asked who made the universe then an answer relative to the intelligence behind the existence of the universe is given.

There is an order to the six elements of total theo-physical understanding, too. *Who* generates *why*, which then motivates *how* from *what*. *Where* and *when* are determined by the purpose behind *what's* existence. This sounds a bit like the famous Abbot and Costello skit, "Who's on First." But, with deeper consideration one finds the elements and order of these elements make perfect sense. It illustrates how religion and speculative philosophy both interact with and support the methodical pursuit of understanding nature and its mechanical functioning.

Religion answers who and why through a methodology similar to the scientific method. It is, however, unbound by the limitations of observed nature like science is. Empiricism is the boundary and base of science, but religion and speculative philosophy is able to go beyond that in answering questions that, in and of themselves, dwell outside the limits of the physical world. In this regard, from the perspective of philosophical science, religion certainly meets the criteria for being labeled a science, in much the same way one would label psychology or theoretical physics as science.

PART TWO

A Rocky Relationship

3

Contemporary Perspectives of Relational Science and Religion

FOR CENTURIES, NO MILLENNIA, humanity has struggled with ideas of faith and the observations of physical science or natural philosophy. Many have sought to separate them and others have proclaimed them as inseparable. From this struggle has come a plethora of theses on the subject. In this book we shall examine the top, or most popular, theses concerning the relationship of religion and science.

Among the top arguments or examinations of theo-scientific relation and interaction are the contradiction thesis, autonomous existence perspective, complimentary interaction perspective, and the unification perspective. For the contradictionist, religion and science are completely incompatible and contradictory to one another while unificationists assert that they work together to define reality as it is experienced by humanity. Between these two views are the concepts of autonomous co-existence and complimentary interaction.

CONTRADICTION THESIS

The original concept of incompatibility between religion and natural science came to its highest level of popularity in the 1800s when it was formally written about by writers John W. Draper and Andrew White.[1] It describes

---

1. It is important to keep in mind that the conflict perspective was held by many scholars for years preceding Draper and White.

and documents the historical clashes between primarily worshippers and primarily explorers, while ignoring the larger population and series of incidents involving those who were both worshippers and explorers.

This thesis states that throughout human history science and religion have been in conflict with each other. It states that neither is able to reconcile or support the other because the ideas produced by each on any given subject are radically opposed to one another. The arguments given in support of this are the beliefs of Middle Ages Christians that the world was flat, the concept of creationism, the opposition to birth control, the alleged prohibition of autopsies, persecution of Galileo, and the erroneous assertion that the rise of Christianity killed ancient science.

Today, many scholars of science, history, philosophy, and theology reject the conflict thesis of the original form. Subsequent research has revealed that religion, more often than not, has been an encouraging influence for scientific research and discovery.[2] Further, institutions of numerous religious movements were responsible for preserving ancient knowledge rather than destroying it. These historical discoveries have proven much of the original conflict thesis to be erroneously based.

For instance, Draper and White assert that religious people during the Middle Ages believed the world was flat.[3] But, this myth was created around the same time as the development of Draper and White's conflict thesis. Records dating from the times of the Middle Ages that contain declarations of a flat world are few and tend to illustrate erroneous thinking rather than accepted fact. The historians David Lindberg and Ronald Numbers wrote, "There was scarcely a Christian scholar of the Middle Ages who did not acknowledge sphericity and even know its approximate circumference."[4]

Although it has been asserted, and remains asserted by a small group today, that religion and science are utterly incompatible, historical and philosophical evidence shows a much different story. The evidence uncovered through a deeper and better examination of the historical interactions between science and religion has led many scholars to reject the contradiction

---

2. Gary Ferngren, editor. *Science & Religion: A Historical Introduction* (Baltimore: Johns Hopkins University Press, 2002).

3. Draper and White. *History of the Conflict between Religion and Science* (London: University College, 1874).

4. David Lindberg and Ronald Numbers. "Beyond War and Peace: A Reappraisal of the Encounter Between Christianity and Science." *Studies in the History of Science and Christianity*. No pages. Online: http://www.asa3.org/ASA/PSCF/1987/PSCF9-87 Lindberg.html.

perspective entirely. There are instances of the religious persecuting scientists and, in contemporary times, of scientists and science faithful persecuting the religious. But, it is not the doctrines and traditions of religion or the discoveries and methodologies of science that have clashed, but rather ignorant and rigid human beings.

AUTONOMOUS EXISTENCE PERSPECTIVE

A more modern view of science and religion has taken form and is described by the likes of Stephen J. Gould and W. T. Stace.[5] Uniquely, each of these two scholars examined the independence perspective, or autonomous existence perspective, from different positions. Gould writes from the scientific side and Stace writes from the philosophy of religion position. Independent of one another, the two concluded in like manner with subsequent scholars confirming their conclusion.

In essence, religion and science are seen as independent sources of knowledge regarding the nature of things, be they physical, spiritual, or conceptual. Their approaches are different but focused on the same goal of universal understanding. Because of this, each discipline has established boundaries or limitations that cannot be crossed without negative consequences. The consequences of philosophical trespass can often be conflict and persecution of one group against another.

According to the autonomous existence perspective (or theory) religion and science co-exist peacefully so long as one does not attempt to infringe upon the other. Further, this view states that science and religion contribute little to nothing to one another because their approaches and standards are so vastly different. They are also overlapping in the examination of all elements of nature and mind. This is a very true but incomplete statement regarding the nature of theo-scientific relations.

There is no doubting that each, science and religion, have limits as to what they can examine and effectively define or provide reliable knowledge about. But, they are not strictly independent of one another because their limits are relative to specific elements of the inquisitive spectrum and are not drawn between perspectives of subject in general. In other words, religion examines certain parts of nature while science examines the remaining parts and a complete understanding comes from the contributed

---

5. Stephen Jay Gould. *Rocks of Ages: Science and Religion in the Fullness of Life* (New York: Ballatine Books, 1999).

information of both. But, the independent existence assertion states that science and religion cover all general aspect of nature from completely different methodologies and mentalities and so long as one does not infringe or opine upon another there is peaceful existence.

COMPLIMENTARY INTERACTION PERSPECTIVE

Many of history's most famous European scientists, including those who have been allegedly persecuted by religious institutions and leaders, claimed to be Christian even though their theories and discoveries were contrary to the declarations of church leadership. Although they differed with the opinions and teachings of church teachers they never once denounced God or criticized Christianity. Why is this? If they were truly in opposition to religion and religious doctrine then why assert a conflicting and provable observation while continuing to praise God?

Contrary to popular belief, scientists of the Middle Ages and during the Age of Enlightenment were not anti-faith or anti-religion. All of them were quite religious within the basic doctrines of Catholicism in Europe. They gave credit to the existence of God and divine intelligence behind the designs of nature. In other cultures there was no difference seen between spiritual and natural enlightenment.

So, why do modern historians and science educators perpetuate the myth of conflict and incompatibility between science and religion? The answer to that question may never be fully understood, but certainly money, politics, greed, and pride are the chief motivators for such erroneous belief. Even in modern times up to 80 percent of scientists in the fields of biology, medicine, and psychology believe there is a supreme being, or God, behind the creation and order of the universe.[6]

The complimentary interaction theory, more commonly referred to as the dialogue perspective, states that science and religion have something to offer the other on all subjects of nature and spirituality. It further states that there is a constant and productive dialogue between scientists and religious leaders that allows for not only peaceful co-existence, but a greater and more complete understanding of nature itself. This is absolutely true in that religion seeks answers to who and why, while science seeks answers

---

6. R. R. Britt, "Scientists' Belief in God Varies by Discipline," Live Science, http://www.livescience.com/379-scientists-belief-god-varies-starkly-discipline.html (accessed July 28, 2012).

to what, when, where, and how. Complete enlightenment then comes from the combined knowledge of scientific and religious inquiry.

In the examination of scientific and religious history, especially in Europe and North America, we find almost every scientist believed in the existence of a creator, intelligent design behind the mechanics of nature, and even life beyond death. Even in modern times there is a large majority of medical science and other natural science scholars who believe in God, divine will, and afterlife. What this indicates is the presence of interactive or dialogue mentality regarding how they viewed religion and its relationship and contributive value to science. This, of course, is in stark contrast to what is taught by modern mainstream scientists and historians.

UNIFICATION PERSPECTIVE

The unification perspective is also known as the integration perspective and deals primarily with the incorporation of science by certain religious sects around the world and throughout history. For instance, Buddhism sees science as a necessary part of reaching ultimate enlightenment and incorporates its findings into its doctrine and traditions. Other religious movements, most notably the less advanced faiths generated by the many sub-cultures of South America and Africa, may reject science and refuse to integrate scientific knowledge into their spiritual reasoning.

But, the integration perspective generally relates that religions have a tendency to encourage scientific inquiry and to incorporate scientific findings into their doctrine and traditions. This is best illustrated through the traditions and teachings of Buddhism where scientific discoveries, if conflicting with contemplative or philosophical conclusions, allow for changes in philosophy that accommodate new scientific information. In fact, Buddhism has a name for this activity of scientific and spiritual integration called *dhamma-vicaya*.

The fourteenth Dalai Lama, Tenzin Gyatso, is well known for spending much of his time with scientists from a wide spectrum of disciplines. In one of his many teachings, or commentaries, on science and religion the Dalai Lama states, "My confidence in venturing into science lies in my basic belief that as in science, so in Buddhism, understanding the nature of reality is pursued by means of critical investigation. If scientific analysis were to conclusively demonstrate certain claims in Buddhism as false then we must accept the findings of science and abandon those claims."[7]

There are, of course, many other religions in the world. Most of them integrate with science to one degree or another. Some are accepting and encouraging, like Buddhism, while others listen but are reluctant to change doctrinal concepts and traditions due to conflicting scientific discoveries. However, all major faiths do and have incorporated science in various forms. It simply takes some longer than others to do so.

Buddhism has been referenced frequently in this work, as it is a great example of a religion that integrates well with science; but what about the other religions? How do they integrate science into their beliefs and traditions? Do they accept science at all? The general answer is that the major world religions do integrate science into their traditions and interpretations regarding the nature of reality and its relation to a creator being and its will. Christianity, Hinduism, Islam, and Judaism are just a few faiths well known for incorporating scientific discoveries into their philosophy and practice. The resistance to modifications in religion due to scientific revelation is a matter of human behavior.

All people are creatures of habit. They are most comfortable in familiar settings, with familiar people, doing routine things. Although humanity does adapt to changes, and certainly has adapted to meet new challenges, it doesn't do so immediately and without some level of resistance. A great example of resistance to and interference caused by sudden changes in routine is in the drive to or from work. Everyone establishes a routine that is followed, quite literally as if controlled by autopilot, when it comes to the repetition of general life, such as leaving home at an established time, driving to school or daycare, and then off to work. But, what happens when there is roadwork or a traffic accident that interferes with that routine?

For most people the sudden and unforeseen delay causes disturbance. Many become angry and their thoughts are interrupted. For most, one disturbance in established routine can generate uncertainty, anxiety, and even frustration. Everything falls behind schedule for that phase of their day, and even when they catch-up they remain a bit discombobulated. This is only a minor routine of individual human behavior. But, what happens on a larger scale—say, the societal or global level of human thought and behavior?

---

7. Dalai Lama. *The Universe in a Single Atom: The Convergence of Science and Spirituality* (New York: Broadway, 2005), 22–40.

Contemporary Perspectives of Relational Science and Religion

One can easily see, and indeed has most likely experienced, the disorienting and frustrating conditions produced when his or her daily routine is interrupted. There is anxiety, irritability, and distracted thought and planning. But, what if the routine isn't individual and has been perpetuated for a century, or even a millennium? These are traditions and routines in behavior that become cultural and deep-seated over many generations. The routines in behavior and belief of individuals revolve around and are usually based on the deeper and broader routines and beliefs of the society to which they belong.

The traditions of society, or cultural unit, are far deeper and far more rigid than those held by individuals. Attempts at instituting changes at this scale or in even expressing an individual or sub-group difference can result in very violent resistance from the authority figures and majority population of the affected society. Whether or not the tradition or long-term belief is religious, scientific, or something else is irrelevant to the fact that human society is slow to change, resistant to changes in routine or established ideology.

It is not inflexibility but rather stiff bending when it comes to cultural traditions and new discoveries, thoughts, perspectives, and changes. There is a form of human rigidity that can hinder progress. It is also this rigidity that allows for the most friction between factions. Even violence can erupt between opposing groups depending on what level of resistance, anger, and perceived threat manifests in the debate. A simple observation that doesn't fit tradition can escalate into debate and on to heated argument and isolated acts of violence quickly, depending on the subject, culture, tradition, discovery, and disturbance generated accepted social norms. From there one might even see organized warfare or civil war within a society.

The integration of science and religion, one to the other, does happen and certainly should happen. But, in the process of this integration or absorption comes friction and painful adjustment for the scientific and religious of the affected culture(s). The hindrance to peaceful interchange and integration of the philosophy of religion with the empirical discoveries of science is not contingent upon religion's traditions or science's discoveries, but on the spiritual and intellectual flexibility of humankind.

4

Atrocities of Both Science and Religion

AS LONG AS HUMANKIND has recorded its own history and advances there has been debate over the positive and negative effects of physical discovery and spirituality. This finger pointing of one group to another brings to mind the old saying that when one points a finger at another he points three back at himself. It seems to illustrate how every human being seeks, almost automatically, to place the blame and responsibility of their failures and ill doings on others.

This chapter is intended to render examples of human intrigue and ill doing and not the evil tendencies of one philosophy or another. In fact, the practices and beliefs generated or learned by humanity are incapable of either good or evil—that is strictly in the domain of human behavior. Religion and the processes of natural science are products of human thought and action, whereas humanity is the source of thought and action. Therefore, it is not man's tools but man himself who is responsible for his suffering.

EUGENICS

Eugenics is a term coined by scientist Sir Frances Galton, cousin to Charles Darwin, in 1883. It is Greek-based and broken down to *eu* (good or well) and *-genes* (born), and quite literally means well-born or of good genetic stock. Galton originally called this area of science *stirpiculture*, but was encouraged to change it after receiving ridicule regarding the term's sexual overtones. The original term also left people with images of animal husbandry rather than of human genetic manipulation.

However, the concept of good and bad lineage and superior human traits existed in the hearts and minds of the aristocracy for centuries prior to Galton. It has long been believed and perpetuated that class was a birthright, and was not achieved or conditioned in a person or people. A prince would never be permitted to marry a common flower girl, nor a merchant's daughter be permitted to marry a farmer's son. There were general beliefs that bringing in "inferior bloodlines" would contaminate superior bloodline. From this, they believed, would come the offspring of undesirable traits and simpleton behavior and intellect. Was this really the reason, though? Did they really believe this or was there more to it?

Of course, there was much more beneath the surface than what was openly presented. What motivated these beliefs and social policies weren't true beliefs in superior and inferior human traits, but a desire to *keep the money and power in the family*. By marrying into other lineages the family of power and wealth was forced to share its wealth with new relatives. They saw this as a threat to both their present and future standing in wealth and societal control.

So great was the greed and power hunger in these elitist families that in-breeding resulted. As far back as the ancient Egyptian empire, the Greek and even Roman history reveals the marrying of first cousins, aunts to nephews, fathers to daughters, and brothers to sisters. The intent was to maintain wealth and power from generation to generation through belief in gifted and superior lineage. The result was genetic degeneration that produced, in short order, children of hideous deformity and mental retardation. This witch's brew of arrogance, greed, ambition, and ignorance produced monstrosities the likes of which are seen only in science fiction horror films today. Instead of preserving they destroyed.

The very name, eugenics, denotes desire for rigid enforcement of societal stratification with emphasis on the higher-class human traits of Western Europe. This is especially so in 1880s Britain where there were rigid caste boundaries and wide gaps between the upper and lower classes. This cultural affliction wasn't restricted to the United Kingdom alone, but was quite present in France, Germany, Italy, Japan, China, India, United States, Canada, Australia, and many other places around the world. It was an attitude of arrogance, greed, and hatred looking for something to justify it, since every major religion certainly condemned it. What, then, did these

Science and Religion

people use to justify the suppression of the majority for the comfort and profit of the few?

The preservation of elite bloodlines got a name from Sir Galton and that name was eugenics. The eugenic concept is not a true science or means of scientific discovery, but rather a justification for elitist attitudes and attempts to maintain wealth and power within the grasp of only a very small group of people. As time went on, though, it began to take on even more sinister meanings that would lead to genocidal murdering on a nearly incomprehensive scale. It would grow to include efforts to achieve and maintain racial purity that included sterilization, euthanasia, abortion, and death camps.

Like a chameleon, the eugenic pseudoscience began to take on a similar appearance to true science as it defined desirable and undesirable human genetic traits. The list of prominent advocates and proponents is shocking to many modern researchers. The list includes but isn't limited to H. G. Wells, Margaret Sanger, Marie Stopes, Theodore Roosevelt, George B. Shaw, John Keynes, John H. Kellogg, Sidney Webb, and Winston Churchill. Adolf Hitler, Himmler, and other German Nazis also believed in eugenics and murdered under the guise of purity preservation.

In the United States there were efforts to institute eugenics socially and governmentally. People with severe mental illnesses or physical deformities were sterilized to prevent perpetuating undesired genes. Strict social standards such as the Jim Crow laws in the south served to prevent romantic and sexual interaction between races so as not to contaminate what they saw as the superior bloodlines. These institutions were cited by Adolf Hitler and Reichsfuhrer Himmler when deciding what to do with Germany's undesirable races and genetic traits. The result was one of the worst atrocities ever recorded in the history of humanity.

Many researchers and historians like to blame eugenics for the atrocities wrought upon so many innocent people. Unfortunately, such blame is both inaccurate and inefficient. Eugenics is a concept derived, designed, and purposed by human beings. It is, therefore, not the source or even the cause of human death and suffering, but the justification used by evil-minded people. Those individuals who killed and harmed others are the ultimate source of atrocities against humanity. Thus, as has been stated many times already, it is humanity that is responsible for humanity's suffering and not its science, philosophy, or religion.

THE CRUSADES

In 1071 C.E. the Seljuk Turks defeated the Byzantine Empire in an alarmingly one-sided war. The emperor of Byzantium, Alexis I, was placed in immediate fear of being completely overrun by the more numerous and capable Turks. In order to acquire both financial and military defensive support, Alexis I appealed to leaders of western kingdoms through their commonality—Christendom. It is here where the beginning of the Crusades is anchored, and it is for this military and political rather than religious reasoning that Jerusalem became a battleground between Muslim East and Christian West.

Alexis used Christian belief as justification for other western kingdoms and the papacy to pick up arms against the Seljuks. The western leaders saw an opportunity to expand their own territories and treasuries through conquest in the Middle East. Thus, Christianity, or the protection of it, became the veil that covered the politics and greed of western monarchs. Alexis I was thinking if fighting broke out in Jerusalem then the Seljuks would be distracted away from the full seizure of Byzantium.

The Muslim leaders were no less guilty of greed and expansionist ambition. Their veil was Islam rather than Christendom, but the goal was the same—achieving more land and more treasure at the expense of their subjects' blood and anguish. There was a mandate regarding the spreading of Islam, but the primary purpose of fighting Christians was to overrun Christian kingdoms and assimilate their lands, resources, and people. Again, pillage and not piety was the motivator among Muslim leaders and the justification for their unprovoked expansionist warfare against the western nations.

Anatolia had been seized in a military attack by the Seljuk Turks and this resulted in cutting access to Jerusalem by European traders. Jerusalem was of both religious and trade importance to the nations of Europe. The saddening truth is that it was more important financially than spiritually. Jerusalem had been under Muslim control for many centuries before the Crusades, and if the Crusades were truly of religious motivation then fighting would have occurred much sooner than it did. Under earlier Muslim control, Jerusalem traded openly with all nations; people of differing faiths and Christian pilgrims were the main tourist income source for Jerusalem's Muslim rulers. Obviously, it was in the interests of both Christians and Muslims to leave the status quo. What happened, then?

Science and Religion

One must look beyond the veils of the Crusade wars and more closely at the conditions and actions that occurred before the call to crusade by the Pope. This pre-action review of history reveals a far different motivation for Western European military action in Palestine. When the battles between the Byzantines and Seljuk forces are examined along with the political and economic desires of Europe it becomes clear that religion was of little thought or presence in the minds of the decision makers, including the imams of Islam and pope of Christianity.

There was a distinct interest in controlling trade routes, enhancing political power, and expanding territory when Europe's leaders answered Alexis' call for assistance as fellow Christians. Although the Byzantine Emperor called for the assistance of Western Europe in the name of Christendom, his actual goal was to pull in allies to stop the Seljuk advance that threatened the very existence of Byzantium. After all, Christendom was not exactly unified in these days, as the western Romans frequently differed and clashed with the Eastern Orthodox. In summary, Alexis was trying to save himself and his empire while Western European nations saw opportunity for expansion in power and wealth. There was no room in the reality of the situation for God, Christ, Allah, or Mohammad.

Religion, for both Muslims and Christians, was nothing more than a justification for the empowered and a manipulation for the commonality of the affected societies. In order to get common people to sacrifice themselves, body and property, the leadership had to find a common purpose under which they would willfully run off to war without regard for self or desire for profit or high payment. The leadership certainly profited in politics and wealth while the commonly led fought and died for the sake and preservation of God or Allah—or so they thought.

Should religion be blamed for the atrocities of Seljuk aggression against Byzantium, or the destruction of Christian religious structures by Fatimid rulers? Should religion be blamed for the near collapse of Byzantium and the greedy intentions of Christian rulers from Western Europe? Is religion the true source of aggression by Muslim and Christian forces or is it a mere excuse used by leaders to justify their actions and manipulate the common masses? Were the common warriors made unaware of the true reason and motivations behind these ghastly campaigns through a mask, or façade, of religious zealotry and hype? The answers to these questions are quite obvious—no. In reality, it is humankind's greed, ambition, and

Atrocities of Both Science and Religion

ignorance and not its religion that led to the bloody series of clashes known as the Crusades.

The greed and ambition of the elite and ruling classes of both the Christian West and Muslim East sought wealth and expanded power. Like an addict, they craved it to a reckless level. The common people, and any others who stood in their way, were of little value. Ordering them to their deaths or ignoring their needs to the point of famine-induced mass death was common in the times of the Crusades.

But, they understood their elitist beliefs were insufficient to take the wealth and power they craved. They also realized they were too few to effectively campaign against any armed resistance. The elite needed the muscle and fighting abilities of their subjects in order to seize and maintain power. The justification then was the common religious conviction that every member of the governed society shared.

Karl Marx, known commonly today as the father of communism, once called religion the opiate of the masses. He placed blame on the faith held by the common people as a mechanism of control that is frequently exploited by the elite ruling class. It was spiritual belief period that Marx opposed and criticized and not one particular faith or another. Marx believed if one were free of religion then one was free of manipulation. The crusades present a perfect example of the exploitation of the common masses through religion and common-sense ignorance by the ruling class.

With all of this having been said one is left with the question of whether or not religion is the cause of the manipulation, the actor, or merely the tool or reasoned justification that facilitates manipulation. Marx is not exactly accurate in labeling religion as the actor of manipulation but is quite accurate in saying that it has been used as a means of manipulation by the ruling class. There are examples of that throughout human history.

Marx is close but not fully accurate. The manipulated are the common masses, the manipulator is the elite ruling class (this is where Marx errs by saying religion is the manipulator), and the means of manipulation (there are many) is the common beliefs, religious or philosophical, of the affected society/culture (the manipulated or influenced). Religion or philosophy isn't the actor, but the tool through which manipulation is accomplished.

But, there is another element to consider: ignorance. The use of Christianity as a justification for violence works only on those who are ignorant to its true and complete teachings and doctrine. In other words, it is easier for contemporary Christians, educated and aware, to refute war in the name of God when it's obvious there are political and economic goals of the leadership, who will profit the most from the accomplishment of those goals. Today's Christians are critical thinkers and more aware of worldly things. This is especially so regarding the understanding of human nature and relations. Today, Christians are better educated in philosophy and politics, have direct access to the Bible in their language, and have actually read and learned the Christian teachings.

The common Christians of the eleventh century C.E. could not read, had no direct access to the Bible, and were taught only what the high priestly class and ruling elite wanted them to know. It is true that illiteracy was prolific even among the middle ranks of the merchant and royal classes. All, except the very highest of the ruling class, were dependent entirely upon the speeches and teachings of the top leadership and bishopric offices. The same situation existed in the eastern Islamic societies. The commoners of Islamic kingdoms were as ignorant of the true teachings of Muhammad as their contemporary Christians were of the teachings of Christ. Their imams and sheikhs told them about Allah and only those parts they wanted them to hear and know.

In all, it was not Christianity, Islam, or Judaism that caused the Crusades or any other conflict fought in the name of one God or another. It was, instead, the greed and ambition of a ruling few, who existed in both the Islamic and Christian camps. The predominant religions of their cultures were used to justify not only the leadership's greed and ambition, but also the brutal acts they ordered and directed to acquire power. Religion is not the cause or encourager of violence, but it has been repeatedly hijacked and misrepresented in order to cover the ill will and doings of a corrupted ruling class.

NAZI GERMANY

The time period in Germany, roughly 1933 to 1945, when Germany was governed by a totalitarian government under the leadership of Adolf Hitler is known among historians as Nazi Germany. For the Jewish community, it is called the Holocaust. This term doesn't merely designate a particular span of time and space for historical reference, though. It is also synonymous with evil and atrociousness of an unprecedented scale.

The National Socialist Workers Party (known as Nazi in its German-based acronym) was the only legal political party in Germany and controlled every aspect of German society and law. Its leader, called the führer, was Adolf Hitler, and its ideology and political doctrine were based on a combination of eugenics, nationalism, and religion. In essence, it pooled general philosophy, religion, and many elements of physical science and pseudoscience in order to define what its members and sympathizers considered the master race, a superior Germanic culture, an absolute Germanic religion, and a need to cleanse the world of lesser humans.

The core leadership of Nazism was comprised of Hitler, Hess, Goebbels, Göring, and Himmler, but even before this group came to power the ideas of racial supremacy and nationalism were professed by many German intellectuals and philosophers. The pseudoscientific principles of eugenics were also widely popular and generally accepted as true throughout Europe. The general population of Germany had been humiliated by their defeat in the First World War and were suffering from an enormous inflation crisis and collapsing economy. The common Germans were desperate and needed solutions. Such were the conditions that they were willing to ignore the suffering of a minority in order to solve the problems of the majority. The country was ripe for manipulation by the likes of the Nazis and its core leadership.

All that was needed in this situation was a couple unifying beliefs and a unifying agent. The beliefs that the German people were a superior human race, that the Jews (both ethnic and theological) were behind Germany's defeat and economic collapse, that the destruction of Judaic control in Germany and Europe would allow the superior Germanic race to stand and conquer the world, and the belief that the German nation was spiritually destined to take over the world were already present in the minds of the average non-Jewish German. What was lacking was a unifying and spiritually motivating speaker like Adolf Hitler and Joseph Goebbels.

In order to attain power and maintain it, the Nazis had to create solutions for the people and better conditions. This is exactly what they did or rather, created an illusion of doing. Their measures were heinous and repulsive to any reasonable person. So, how did they manage to not only create but execute the solution to the "Jewish Problem?" How did they get so many *reasonable* people to do what *reasonable* people normally refuse to do or even consider? They justified the evil through economic, social, political, scientific, and religious means. These alleged justifications for the atrocities committed by the German regime allowed for individuals to act without guilt, blame, or personal responsibility—so they thought, anyway.

Science and Religion

Economically, the Nazis pointed out how the banks, large business, and means of production were all controlled by the Jewish citizens of Germany. It was claimed that German and European Jews were helping other Jews and harming the greater population of non-Jewish German citizens by withholding loans, investments, and charging outrageous amounts for goods. This was only propagated by the Nazis, but was not invented by them. Though it was a very false belief, it was held by a large volume of the greater German and European population. The Nazis simply preached it and by doing so they provoked resentment and hatred in the minds of the non-Jewish German population. The Nazi Party was sympathetic to biased beliefs held by desperate people and they, in turn, began to see the Nazis as allies in their social struggle.

Socially, the Nazis played on another commonly held, prejudiced belief. This belief held that the entire world population of Jews was conspiring to overthrow governments and enslave non-Jewish people. They claimed to have found secret documents that laid out plans and plots against the world's non-Jewish people. This claim is clearly outrageous to contemporary people living in relatively normal and sustaining economies and environments, but for the starving, homeless, and economically desperate people of Germany this was a fact to be feared and eliminated. The Nazi party played on that and won support, sympathy, and loyalty from the German people and Germanic peoples of Poland and Austria. Being hailed as knights fighting evil dragons, the people grew a sense of pride, purpose, and unified determination that was exploited and manipulated by the Nazi leadership.

Politically, the Nazis claimed several things that were also held by the majority German population. One of these claims was that the German government was being controlled and exploited by Jewish politicians and their sympathetic allies. Another was that the failure of the German Armed Forces in the First World War was because the Jews in political power in Germany conspired with Jews in Russia and France to ensure the great Germanic race did not succeed or grow. Again, these are truly outrageous and unfounded claims. But, the majority of non-Jewish Germans held beliefs of this sort to be true. And, like all other desperation-rooted social beliefs, the Nazis preached it and pledged to stop it. Through this they gained allegiance and support from the German masses.

The people became convinced there was a worldwide conspiracy within the Jewish faith to control governments, suppress non-Jews, seize all wealth, and eventually kill all non-Jews. In a morbid twist, the Nazis would use this to justify the seizure of political power, control of economic process, seizure of wealth, social manipulation, warfare, and even mass murder. They would do exactly what they claimed the Jews were planning to do to them.

It was the mass murdering, the industry of death instituted by Nazi Germany, that required the justifications found in science and pseudoscience. It takes quite a bit of rationalizing to get people to do things as horrendous as what took place in the concentration camps. Genetics and eugenics became the modeling mechanisms from which the belief of racial superiority became an illusionary fact. But, that was all it was, nothing more than an illusion designed to allow individuals to believe the heinous acts they did were right and moral—*endeavors of evil meant for some greater good.*

Even the pseudoscience of phrenology was used to demonstrate the genetic inferiority of Jews and other undesirables. These faux sciences justified euthanizing the mentally ill and physically deformed. The same was used to justify killing homosexuals and people of odd sexual practices. Marriage and reproduction was dictated with harsh consequences for violators. Jews were identified as both genetically and socially inferior and thus their murder was a conclusion intended by design. The Nazi party and government misused and misrepresented science in order to justify and encourage the killing of well over six million innocent people. After all, they killed more than just Jews during that time and they used twisted science to justify it.

Religion was also seized and twisted in order to justify and encourage the acts of racism, violence, conquest, murder, and theft. The Nazis pointed out to the majority Lutheran and Roman Catholic Germans that it was Jews who crucified Christ and condemned him. They harped on the fact that Jesus of Nazareth was tried, convicted, and executed not by the Romans, but by the Jews in Jerusalem. This stirred up resentment in spite of Jesus's teachings to forgive. In addition to this, they also claimed Jewish-controlled banks and charities were spending huge amounts of money on the expansion of Zionism and in the smothering out of Christianity. This, too, generated tremendous resentment and tied other unfounded biases into the mix.

How did the Nazi regime manage to convince the majority German population that Jewish people were their enemies, they were destined to rule the world, and they were a superior human race? How did they get average and reasonable people, in the millions, to abandon their ethical

Science and Religion

and theological convictions? Did science really support the claims and actions of Nazi Germany? Did the common religions of the region predispose people to killing Jews and other undesirables within their culture? A paragraph of questions can be answered in five words: misrepresentation, misuse, desperation, ignorance, and exploitation.

The people were not predisposed to hate through religion or social ethics, but they were desperate, poor, and ignorant, which made them vulnerable. Their vulnerability was exploited by the Nazis through misrepresentation of facts, misuse of science, and misuse and misrepresentation of religion. A hungry person will give up his or her freedom and will abandon his or her moral values in order to eat, and the ignorant person is oblivious to the reality behind the illusion. Those who are hopeless gravitate towards anything that gives them hope and a sense of purpose. This was identified and used to manipulate a demoralized and desperate Germany by the core leadership of the Nazi Party, and they gained power through it.

Neither the principles of science nor the philosophies of religion caused or even encouraged the atrocities of Nazi Germany. They are products of human thought, exploration, and belief and are at the mercy of human interpretation and application. Neither of these two elements of human understanding are responsible for the Holocaust as they were misused, ignored, twisted, and misrepresented by humans of twisted and evil intent. Therefore, religion didn't cause or justify Nazi atrocity any more than science, but rather humans rationalized and committed these atrocities against other humans, and those ill-intended humans are responsible entirely.

Jihad

The term "jihad" has been in existence in the teachings and practices of Islam since its inception by the prophet Mohammad. In its original use, jihad represented a spiritual and psychological struggle against those ways, thoughts, and deeds that were defined as sinful within the Islamic faith. Jihad, therefore, is intended to be a struggle to maintain spiritual righteousness and purity. It is a struggle every person makes everyday regarding what's right and wrong in the eyes of Islam's god, Allah. It is a form of internal warfare whereby the individual fights against sin and evil within him or herself.

Atrocities of Both Science and Religion

Unfortunately, the term jihad has taken on a more sinister and deadly definition by radical and violent followers of contemporary Islam. Starting as early as the 1970s C.E., Islamic political and theocratic leaders have morphed the meaning of jihad to suit their purposes of conquest and expansion. Imams have given sermons and blessings to organizations designed to commit heinous acts of violence against innocent people in the name of Islam and/or Allah. Spiritual jihad has been redefined to mean armed and violent warfare against all who are not Muslim. Even this is not specific enough as each faction of Islam believes the others are blasphemers; they issue death warrants against them too.

This, Islam, is a point of confusion for many when deciding whether or not religion is the cause of human violence and suffering. This is because Islam was created and expanded through a seemingly constant series of battles and wars. Mohammad, the founder of Islam, is well known for personally leading many of these early battles. There are statements throughout the Qur'an and Hadith that address forced conversion and violence against non-believers. In one spot we read there should be no compulsion in religion, and in another place we read Islam should be spread by the sword. Thus, the religious directives concerning such things as expansion, conversion, and preaching can be and are interpreted in opposing applications from one imam or faction to another.

The question of whether Islam is an example of religion-caused human violence, self-destruction, and suffering remains. It can, at times, appear unclear. So, which is it? Does Islam encourage and preach violence or is it misinterpreted and misrepresented? The answer to this is it depends on who is interpreting and applying it and what their goals are.

This then, puts Islam in the same boat as all other religions. Though it was born in a world of violence, Islam's earliest doctrines and teachings are of peace, love, and compassion for others. It isn't until later that Mohammad, a very real and imperfect human, begins to speak in terms of forced conversion and warfare in the name of Allah. The peaceful parts of Islam, those believed to have been taught to Muhammad by Gabriel, are often ignored and trampled upon by people in positions of power or in positions seeking power. This is not unlike what humanity has done to every other religion across the world and throughout time.

Groups such as Quds Force (Iranian-backed Shia terror group), Hamas (Iranian-backed Shia terror group in Palestine), and Al Qaeda (international Islamic terror organization) use the mutated definition of Jihad to justify their bombings, kidnappings, and terrorizing of others to achieve political, financial, social, or religious goals. Bombing an Israeli school bus full of children is often done in the name of Islam through the erroneous and perverted use of the term, jihad. It is not in religion's name or for a holy cause that these individuals fight and kill, but for the sole purpose of personal gain and power.

Contemporary, armed jihad is a perversion of the original spiritual jihad. This perversion comes not from the true teachings of Islam, but from the fact twisting of power hungry and militant-minded Islamic leaders and radicals. Therefore, it is not the religion of Islam that promotes warfare and violence against others, but the human desire to force politics upon other people and cultures that promotes and leads death to the doors of the innocent.

People, especially those undereducated, are easier to motivate through spiritual causes than through general reasoning. So, leadership remakes religion to fit their agenda and the ignorant accept it without question or consideration. In this case, too, there is no blame to be put upon the religion of Islam, but upon those greedy and ambitious leaders who twisted the faith and misled others to suit their violent and greedy purposes.

NUCLEAR, BIOLOGICAL, AND CHEMICAL WEAPONS

Nuclear, biological, and chemical weapons have got to be the most vile things ever invented and used by humankind. These weapons of mass destruction (WMD) and a favorite for terrorists are commonly known by the acronym, NBC. These weapons have been responsible for not just a few deaths and injuries per use, but rather thousands of deaths and injuries per use. Biological weapons are the first to have been used in hostile action by one group against another. That was followed by the use of deadly chemicals. Finally, nuclear weapons and their ability to kill in the hundreds of thousands, and even millions, came.

What exactly is a biological weapon? It is the intentional introduction or infection of a selected population with dangerous microbes, bacteria, viruses, and/or parasitic organisms. The intent behind this deliberate exposure to dangerous parasites and pathogens is to cause death and severe disability to a large population of people. Bio-weapons are horrible in their effect as the agent is usually incurable, difficult to detect, fast acting, and painful to the afflicted. They also spread exponentially from person to

Atrocities of Both Science and Religion

person without distinguishing between combatants and non-combatants or adults and children.

Diseases such as small pox, bubonic plague, and anthrax are commonly weaponized by various military organizations around the world. In most cases, the weaponization process for these diseases is relatively easy. In fact, most can be mass-produced in a simple college biology laboratory. They can be delivered to target population in many ways, too. An infected courier can be sent into the targeted population, food or water supply can be contaminated, or it can be disbursed through artillery and air through a small explosion or even sprayed over a targeted area by a crop-duster aircraft.

The worst WMD is most often considered the bio-weapon. The reason for this distinction is it is easy to get, inexpensive to produce, very mobile, and cheap to deploy. That makes this the easiest for poorer governments and terrorist organizations to get a hold of. A common nickname for bio-weapons is "the poor man's nuke."

Not only is it cheap, but biological warfare has been used for centuries and is proven effective in war and terror. One of the earliest known accounts of the use of germs as a weapon occurred during the siege of Fort Pitt, Pennsylvania in July 1763.[1] Indians in the Pittsburgh area surrounded the fort, and Lord Jeffery Amherst, commanding British Forces, issued blankets infected with small pox to the besieging Indians surrounding the fort.[2] The result was an epidemic that nearly wiped out the native population in the area. Men, women, and children, non-combatant and combatant, were all infected and killed by the disease.

Another example of germ warfare can be seen in World War II when the Japanese dropped tons of fleas, infected with bubonic plague, on Chinese civilians in Northern China between 1940 and 1942. The result is an estimated 240,000 human fatalities. Most of these fatalities were civilian women and children. The massive amount of death caused by a series of airborne deployments is what gives the bio-weapon the nickname "poor man's nuke."

The next oldest and equally easy to make WMD is chemical weapons. These weapons use chemicals of various forms to cause serious physical

---

1. Elizabeth A. Fenn, "Biological Warfare in Eighteenth-Century North America: Beyond Jeffery Amherst," *The Journal of American History*, March 2000, 86:4.

2. Howard H. Peckham, *Pontiac and the Indian Uprising* (Chicago: University of Chicago Press, 1947), 226.

harm or death to humans exposed to them. There are several types of chemical agents in place like nerve agent, blood agent, blister agent, and irritants. Chemicals such as mace, oleoresin capsicum (OC) spray, and CS gas (tear gas) are all chemical weapons of the irritant, non-lethal type. Chemicals that burn the skin and exposed mucus membranes like chlorine gas and mustard gas belong to the blister agent branch of chemical weapons. Blister agents cause severe burns, cause blindness, and often result in death. Nerve agents consist of chemicals designed to attack the human central nervous system and death usually results from asphyxiation as respiration and heart rate are neurologically interrupted and shut down. Blood agents prevent red blood cells from holding and delivering oxygen throughout the body resulting in an agonizing death by suffocation.

Chemical weapons are by far the easiest and cheapest to manufacture, store, maneuver, and deliver. Like bio-weapons, chemical weapons can be delivered through a wide spectrum of means such as artillery air burst, aircraft dispersal, food and water contamination, aerosol release, and ground-level explosive. The shelf life of chemical weapons is far longer than bio-weapons, too.

The most famous, or infamous, uses of chemical weapons occurred during World War I when chlorine gas filled artillery shells and landmines were used extensively on both sides of the conflict. Those who survived exposure to these agents suffered permanent and agonizing damage to the respiratory system, skin, and eyes. Many were permanently blinded by mustard and chlorine gas exposure. On March 20, 1995, nerve agent Sarin and VX gas were used on a Tokyo subway by a terrorist group in Japan known as Aum Shinri Kyo (meaning, supreme truth).

On August 6, 1945 and again on August 9, 1945 the United States brought an entirely new form of weapon into the world. The Japanese cities of Nagasaki and Hiroshima were both completely destroyed along with the vast majority of their residents when nuclear bombs were detonated over each one. This was the first time, and only time to date, that nuclear weapons have been used in military conflict. In the immediate blast area nothing survived, the shadows of people were burned into the concrete walls and steps of buildings and all wooden structures were burned to ash. Almost all of the residents of these two cities were civilian non-combatants and neither city held any significant military importance.

A minimum of 45,000 people were killed immediately upon detonation of a single bomb over Hiroshima with an estimated total of 166,000 dead less than two months following the bombing. One bomb killed 166,000 people in Hiroshima alone with another 60,000 to 80,000 dead in Nagasaki. Two bombs dropped over two cities managed to kill over half a million people before the end of two months.

Yes, WMDs are products of scientific research and applied scientific knowledge and it is easy to initially think science is the reason for their existence and the atrocities they have wrought upon the earth and its inhabitants. But, such an assumption would be enormously incorrect and place responsibility upon the shoulders of the wrong thing. Science, like religion, is only a tool—a methodical approach to an empirical understanding of nature. It does not think or act on its own. It cannot even apply itself, as science is inquiry and there is no inquiry where there is no inquirer.

Science is to humanity as a wrench is to a mechanic—a mere tool. How the tool is used and what results from its use are dependent upon the actions and will of its wielder. In the case of the wrench, one can do good by tightening a bolt that stops a leak or do bad by striking another over the head. In the case of nuclear science, one can do great things such as generate efficient power, create treatments for cancer, or offer medicinal imaging, or one can do heinous things such as build a nuclear bomb and drop it on a population. The result, good or bad, is dependent upon two things—the tool and the actor.

In view of this realization, one must conclude it is people who exercise and apply science, which makes people responsible for the consequences of such application. Science is a methodical quest for knowledge and nothing more, while applied science is the use of knowledge and nothing less. It is humanity only who determines what is studied and how the resulting knowledge is applied. Therefore, the misuse and abuse of the knowledge gained through scientific experimentation and exploration is committed not by itself but by humans, and when that misuse results in human suffering then the blame stands not with science but with other elements of humanity.

PART THREE

A Truly Perfect Union

5

Religion: Venerator and Giver of Hope

RELIGION HAS A VERY distinct individual and social role to fulfill. In fact, there is more than one pair of shoes to wear for religion. It is irrelevant as to which form of religion is in place when considering the needs religious belief and practice achieve for the individual and the collective, cultural mind. There are needs regarding particular uncertainties in life for both the individual and the group elements of humanity that are answered through religion and religious practice and cannot be answered, satisfied, or soothed by any other means—including science.

There are a plethora of questions that cannot be satisfactorily answered by the mechanics and empiricism of science or by the elements observed by the naked and unaided eye. There are so many things in this universe that seem to defy our senses and the logic of science. Science is a tool that has answered many questions of the natural and measurable world, but there are things that seem to stretch beyond nature and into that realm we like to call supernatural (beyond the rules of nature).

Even in the science of psychology we learn the mind cannot be seen or measured and thus it is behavior, outward behavior, that is observed, measured, and experimented with. It is interesting to note that the term "psychology" is derived from the two Latin words *psyche*, meaning soul or mind, and *logia*, meaning to possess knowledge of or study. Quite literally, the first meaning of the word psychology came in its Latin use of *psychologia*, which meant the study of the soul. Today, of course, it means the study of behavior and not the soul or mind. Soul and mind remain in the realms of general and religious philosophy. Why is this?

Science and Religion

The science of psychology can only observe, understand, predict, and control external behavior. It is very limited to the study of the mechanics of thought processing and not the nature of the mind or soul. We can say we sense a soul and our minds are separate from the body, but we cannot directly observe or experience it through the other five standard senses. Yet, we all know it is there.

Science, at present, cannot adequately explain this sensing of a second reality whose abode is just beyond the grasp of the laws of the physical universe. It isn't a part of the nature that is studied by the many disciplines of science, and thus it exists but outside of what is generally understood and defined to be nature. The soul and the essence of mind, then, are elements of the supernatural and to understand them requires an entirely different approach than what science or common sensation can provide or even allow. The different approach used to understand the mind and soul is made through general and spiritual philosophy (religion).

Spiritual encounters, experience, and even intervention are believed to happen on a regular basis by a significant amount of the world's population. These experiences, which stand well outside the boundaries of natural processes and laws, are part of the experiencing party's reality. The absence of such experience(s) becomes part of human reality, too. Thus, human reality is a product of sensation, perception, and interpretation of information as a whole and not of individual little pieces. "The whole perceptual experience exceeds the sum of its parts."[1]

If the spiritual, supernatural event is experienced by more than one person then it is a part of confirmed individual and group experience. The below example illustrates how one person's experience and interpretation of reality is confirmed by another.

Jim: "Did you see that?"

Michael: "I sure did!"

Of course, this is a very simple and preliminary example of experience and interpretive confirmation by and between two or more people. Experiential confirmation will go further than this initial question-and-answer moment, though. In all cases, the eyewitnesses to an event, spiritual or otherwise, will discuss the details, place some form of meaning to the elements of the experience, and come to a consensus as to what the totality of the experience is and what it means.

---

1. Max Wertheimer. "Study on Figural Organization." Lecture, Frankfurt University, 1923.

Religion: Venerator and Giver of Hope

Accuracy regarding the laws of nature in matters of supernatural or unusual experience is not as important as the consensus of meaning applied to the experience. Naturally, this is a type of thinking and acceptance that cannot be restrained by the process of scientific inquiry and analysis. In some cases it may even challenge the principles of common sense. After all, common sense is based on a natural pattern of cause-and-effect experience,[2] and when something steps outside the rules of nature it also stands aside from any patterns in nature.

Rene Descartes would say that the concept of God is placed into our minds by God itself,[3] while David Hume would say that the God concept is a mere construct based on a pattern of human experiences.[4] Regardless of the perspective one may accept regarding the origin of the concept or belief in God, the fact is there is a belief or concept of God acknowledged or inferred in both perspectives. These two philosophers, and many others, seem fixed on where the idea came from rather than if it is or isn't. Why can it not be both?

We are all created through both biological and spiritual processes. It stands to reason that the one who creates would leave information imprinted within the created. Thus, the concept of God comes from God and is within us all from birth. But, there is more than that to the story. As we grow and live from one year to the next we experience more and more things that we keep tucked away for future reference. Many of these experiences become part of the patterns of nature we depend on in routine daily life while other experiences aren't easy to classify or tuck away in memory processing.

These are the experiences that stand alone and apart from the routines and predictability of nature and seem to even defy the laws and rules that govern the physical world around us. Because these events and experiences stand outside the norms of nature, we struggle to find meaning in them. Such experiences can be either frightening or soothing, depending on the meaning assigned to the event by the observer. Many of these experiences serve to support or enhance the God concept already present within us. In other words, God created man who knows God through the touch of his

---

2. David Hume, "An Enquiry Concerning Human Understanding." Section II: Of the Origin of Ideas. 1748.

3. Rene Descartes, *Meditations of First Philosophy. Meditation III.* 1641.

4. David Hume, "An Enquiry Concerning Human Understanding." Section II: Of the Origin of Ideas. 1748.

Science and Religion

creator but is confirmed in God through his experiences in life that stretch beyond the norms of nature.

When people consider their own innate sense of God's existence with their accumulated experiences that clearly indicate the presence and intervention activities of God they find individual or internal confirmation of both the existence and presence of God. What is confirmed in the mind and soul isn't necessarily the God of Christian definition, but a basic definition of divineness, perfection, omnipotence, and superior being. Also in this realization is an automatic acknowledgement that there must be a realm, world, or universe that runs parallel to that universe we see and experience physically throughout our biological lives.

When others have similar individual experiences and the same sense of divine existence they speak with and compare thoughts with others. When a consensus of meaning, understanding, and interpretation is reached there is present a group or social confirmation of spiritual belief. In this level of shared spiritual interpretation and belief the seed of organized religious expression and practice is planted. It is a well-known and easily observed social phenomenon for like-minded people to gravitate towards, interact with, and create social and cultural structures that reinforce their bonds and promote their shared beliefs.

Where the various sciences say little about what happens after the body dies, other than decomposition processes, religion renders explanation and continuance of consciousness. All people want to see a better and happier time in their lives and without hope the normal response is to give up. It is very discouraging and depressing to believe one ceases to exist in any form upon the death of the body. In fact, such despair can be so great that a person will stop eating, halt activities, dwindle, and slowly die. A person without hope will often ask him or herself, "why bother?" Suicide notes are often loaded with expressions of despair and hopelessness.

So, what does religion do that science cannot? Religion acknowledges the realm of existence that stands well outside the natural universe to which science is restricted. It acknowledges the imprinted knowledge of a superior creator being. It incorporates special experiences as confirmation of a world beyond this one and of the existence of not just the biological body, but of a spiritual consciousness that moves and exists independent of the body. If one were to have these conclusions and beliefs in mind, then one can plan on a future that goes beyond his or her lifetime; there is a purpose behind his or her existence other than eventual death, and there is justified hope that conditions in life quality will improve and suffering will be eliminated. This hope then gives motivation to live better, overcome hardship, innovate, care about how one impacts the lives of others, and look forward to and plan for the future—even that future that lay beyond the individual's expected biological lifespan.

Spiritual belief, or religious conceptualization, renders humanity with an appreciation for both those things that are of nature and those things that originate in the supernatural. Along with a sense of purpose and hope, humanity also learns and appreciates that all life is a creation of the divine creator and they are, therefore, special creatures serving a deliberate, designed purpose and divine will of a different scope. Each living thing, on earth and upon those worlds we have yet to discover, is a precious creation of the divine, and thus they must be respected and protected as humanity would respect and protect itself. When humankind examines its environment it realizes there is exceptional beauty, creativity, and intelligent direction behind the mechanical interactions of the various ecosystems and environments in which known life flourishes.

Humanity's experiences with the various forms of life and natural processes that surround it allow for a certain appreciation of what has been made by that who makes. Through this appreciation and admiration comes a desire to venerate and honor not only the created, but the creator too. Some people even find themselves drawn in to a closer examination of life and natural processes—the inquisitors of science emerge.

Thus, humankind is given two great things by and through religion and spiritual awareness. The first is hope and the second is appreciation and veneration of all that is, by that which has created. Through our very creation comes the basic awareness of the existence of God who intercedes in ways that render experiences reinforcing this awareness of the divine. In knowing God humankind also knows of the universe beyond the natural and observable universe, and this allows for an awareness of self as both biological and spiritual being. One then gains hope for the future and release from the permanence of death through the realization the spiritual self will survive the death of the biological self. Humanity appreciates life and nature and venerates the creator of these, who also created humanity.

6

Science: Discoverer and Giver of Comfort

SCIENCE IS THE MOST important vessel by which humanity gathers knowledge about the natural world. It is a product of human inquiry and exploration that has occurred over many thousands of years. Today's science and, more specifically, today's scientific method have resulted in the unraveling of many mysteries. It has advanced our understanding of the mechanisms and means of nature's course and allowed us to use that understanding to build new things, improve the quality of life, and even extend the human expected life span. We learn how everything works through a systematic and time-tested methodology.

Certainly, science tells us how things in the natural world work: how we breathe, why it's necessary, what it affects in our body, and so on. The same can be said for science: how does it work, where does it occur, what is it, and how does it interact with all the other elements of nature? It isn't all mathematical and mechanical, though. There are other forms of discovery that are followed.

In geography, for instance, there is a need to physically observe and explore the terrain and oceans of earth. Through this scientific discipline we have an accurate mapping and understanding of the earth's land and oceanic attributes. From the geographer follows the biologist who finds and catalogs new life forms around the globe through fieldwork. At the same time, scientists are not only explainers and contemplators, but also explorers and discoverers. Botanists and chemists will work together in order to study new plants and discover their medicinal properties.

Science: Discoverer and Giver of Comfort

Science is a train racing down the track of discovery, propelled by the application of knowledge. It is in the core of human nature to be curious and investigate the properties, origins, and mechanics of the universe around us. The development of a methodical, empiricist, and investigative approach is simply a reasonable outcome to such a human trait.

Proclaiming science is wrong or bad is to declare humanity wrong or bad. It is probably, or most likely, a combination of the two depending on the disposition of the person and his or her application of scientific knowledge. Thus, science and the knowledge it generates for humanity is neither good nor evil. When used properly by those of the appropriate mindset and intent, science can achieve great things for humanity and beyond. When used improperly by people of ill disposition and intent, science then achieves atrociousness and great evil. The effect of science is a function of its application by humanity.

There is no doubting humanity has achieved many great things through scientific inquiry and the application of its resulting understandings and discoveries. The greatest and most productive achievements seem to lie in the area of medical science. It is in this area of scientific research and wisdom that cancers have been defined, their causation identified, and remedies developed and honed. The same is said for viral and bacterial threats to human health. There was a time when the average human life span was just a little beyond forty years. Today, thanks to advances in a wide spectrum of scientific inquiry the average human life span in the United States is well beyond seventy years.[1]

In addition to the advances in medicine are advances in literally everything from the clothing we wear to the means by which we communicate. Machines and computers have eased the need for intensive labor to achieve higher productivity levels. Science and engineering have not only improved conditions for the farmer but chemists, biologists, and geneticists have managed to find ways to triple crop outputs, reduce damage by pests, and increase drought endurance. Without these advances, brought about through scientific research and applied scientific findings, feeding the ever-increasing human population on earth would be impossible.

The areas of nature that are, at present, outside the direct control or manipulative skills of humanity are studied intensely. For instance, weather cannot yet be controlled through the application of scientific knowledge,

---

1. U.S. Dept. of Health, National Vital Statistics Reports, Vol. 59, Number 9, September 2011, 2.

but it is understood well enough, through the application of the scientific method, to allow governments, communities, and individuals to prepare for weather-related disasters. Understanding the nature of weather has reduced fatalities and even property damage through the development of better structures and preventative measures. Where these efforts fail there exists evacuation and rescue plans and resources.

When we examine science and all of its good products we find that, when used properly by right-minded people, humanity is handed great comfort, understanding, advancement in technology, and longevity in life. At one time, humans lived in small tribes and inside caves, but now they live in aboveground structures that provide significant protection from wildlife and the elements while enhancing individual physical comfort. Rocks were once the chairs and couches of Paleolithic man, but modern man has fabric-covered and stuffed cushion chairs and couches today. That's an astounding advancement in human casual comfort alone.

Through our natural inquisitiveness came an accumulation of knowledge that was modified, honed, and added to by subsequent generations. Where there is great argument concerning the physical evolution of humankind there is absolute agreement in regards to humanity's evolution in knowledge and wisdom. History reveals that each generation has built on the knowledge and wisdom of the preceding generation—humanity has evolved from primitive to modern man in knowledge and wisdom, at the very least. Where history shows stifled or suppressed inquisitiveness there is also stagnation in human advancement of knowledge and technology.

Is there a conflict between the efforts and discoveries of science and the venerations and traditions of faith and religion? In short, no, there is no conflict in fact, but rather in the minds and mindsets of the individuals involved with their comparison. Science explores, defines, and analyzes those things that are observable or otherwise detectable in the physical universe (the natural world) while religion (Christian or otherwise) explores, defines, and analyzes those things that are sensed, unseen, and lie outside or beyond rules of the physical universe (the supernatural world). Science covers the elements of the natural world while religion covers those topics of the supernatural world.

Still, there are those who will cling to science and condemn faith while others cling to faith and condemn science. These are people who have difficulty understanding there is an equal but opposite side to all things. There is the seen and tangible, as well as the unseen yet sensed or deduced. These people see only in black and white while there are many colors around them. Such a condition can afflict he who sees only the observable and mathematically explainable or she who sees the spirit in things and a great plane of existence from which all other things have come. But, neither can see the whole picture of reality, which is comprised of two parts—the physical or natural and the non-physical or supernatural. Rigidity, not openness, is what gives rise to condemnation, regardless of position or perspective.

Conclusion

Science and Religion Combined as the Greater Whole of Human Understanding and Advancement

THERE IS A CONSISTENT theme permeated thoroughly throughout this book. That theme is twofold and incorporates the realization that there is no conflict between science and religion, but rather there exists a form of complimentary co-existence, and it is man and not his inquisitive means or spiritual understanding that is at fault for the infliction of suffering upon others. These are the two main ideas that have surfaced through statement, comparison, narrative, and illustration throughout this work.

Rigidity is the reason people fail to see the truth that stands before them. These people are restricted to a polar position of one perspective or the other and are unwilling to incorporate the other, equal but different view of nature. When faced with a glimpse of the other side, or the other half of the "whole picture," they tend to reject it and may even go so far as to act violently to suppress this other way of seeing things. This rigidity is not constrained to only one side of reality's whole, but depending on the individual it can exist on either end of the spectrum.

In order to understand where humanity has gone wrong with its perceptions of science and religion one must first examine what they are individually and what they create when combined in application to our experiences and the phenomena of the natural and supernatural worlds. It is essential that science and religion be identified and classified correctly, as human tools, in order that the reality of human condition can be seen in its raw and total form. Otherwise, humankind simply sees and understands half of what is going on physically and spiritually. It is not the restricted viewing of reality that leads to conflict between the inquisitors and advocates of science and those of faith and spiritual awareness.

Humanity is at fault for the bad and credited for the good. Humans, all of us, do not like to admit wrongdoing or take personal responsibility for the consequences of wrongdoing. We certainly would not need attorneys if the case were otherwise. When people win a race, achieve a great academic goal, bring peace to a region of the world, or invent some medical marvel that lengthens the human lifespan they are quick to take credit for it and even jealously guard that credit. But, when people kill, persecute, harass, ostracize, discriminate, withhold charity, or wage brutal war they are quick to justify their actions and lay blame on others. The bottom line is we do not like to take responsibility for our ill doings and will go to great lengths to avoid responsibility.

What do we hear from our brothers and sisters when good is done? We hear, "I won the race," "I achieved this goal," and "I brought peace." What do we never hear them say? We never hear them say: "Thank God for giving me the strength to when this race." "Thanks to my scientific knowledge of human anatomy and biochemistry, I have won this race." "Thank you, Lord, for bringing this success to me." "I am thankful for the scientific method that allowed me to make this discovery." We never give credit to God or science when things are good for us and we have done well. We always take full credit for it while casting both science and religion aside.

What is heard when one kills another, steals from another, wages war and murder against others, or withholds much-needed charity from others? "I killed him because he offended Islam!" "We waged war to free the Holy City from the Muslim infidels!" "I took their things because they are an inferior race and science supports this." "We took their land and trinkets because they were ignorant and weak in trusting us and we wanted their things." "We waged war against the Jews because they are liars and snakes and offend God." "Scientific data proves Iraq is producing and hording weapons of mass destruction." Can you see how both science and religion are being used to justify the evil side of humanity?

What does all of this mean? What conclusions should be drawn from these observations—these realizations regarding human nature and character and the universe? The examples listed here are not alone, either. There are not thousands but millions of examples throughout the history of humankind where atrocities and ill doings have been done under the false justification of religion, science, or both. Science and religion do not kill people; people kill people.

Like a coin, humans have two sides. We are designed with a duality of good and evil. Not one of us is spared this duality, though one has been born absent of evil (Jesus Christ) and others have been able to meditate away their darker side (the Buddhist and Hindus). We are proud of the lighter side and ashamed of the darker side. Thus, we all seek praise for being good and receive gratification through doing good while we seek to shed responsibility for our evil side and feel ashamed for our darker deeds. In order to evade personal responsibility for our sinful, unethical, and immoral ways we use religion and science to rationalize and justify them.

Therefore, it is humanity that is responsible for humanity's suffering and not its religion or methodology for discovering the laws of nature. It is greed, covetousness, lust, desire for power, political ambitions, and intolerance that has led to the atrocities recorded throughout history. Science and religion have been nothing more than tools for the justification of these immoral and wicked doings. The cause, all along, has been human beings and their uncontrolled darker side combined with their rejection of personal responsibility for wrongful ways. Our constructs and conceptualizations are not responsible—we are.

In order for humanity to acquire complete knowledge and understanding of the environment in which it exists there must be balanced understanding of the natural and supernatural worlds. Seeing only half the picture leaves people confused and without ability to draw sense out of what they see and calculate. But when religion—a means of understanding those things that lie outside of the laws and confines of nature—and science—the means by which humankind explores and discovers the mechanics and nature of the physical realm—come together in a single or group mind then the full enlightenment of reality unfolds and becomes clear.

Perhaps it is this united perspective that leads to the nirvana spoken of in Buddhist traditions? Common perceptions of the universe through a joint physical and metaphysical means surfaces when examination of all religious practices and constructs is made. In fact, the most commonly shared belief between all religions is that there is both a spiritual and physical universe in which body and soul exists.

Regardless of which means is favored by the human observer the fact remains that religion tends to motivate, comfort, and assure while science explores, questions, tests, and defines. They are tools whose functions are

Conclusion

related only when they are combined and applied jointly to the many questions we ask. In all other respects these two tools of mind and intellect do not cross paths. Though many see them as competitors and try to force their paths to cross, the reality is they are incapable of conflict. Conflicting conclusions and beliefs are the products of human contemplation and observation and are not rooted in faith or science.

www.ingramcontent.com/pod-product-compliance
Lightning Source LLC
Chambersburg PA
CBHW050831160426
43192CB00010B/1985